Rescued from the Sea
An Archaeologist's Tale

Clive Waddington

Published by Archaeological Research Services Ltd, Angel House, Portland Square, Bakewell, Derbyshire , DE45 1HB, United Kingdom.

and

Northumberland Wildlife Trust Ltd, Garden House, St Nicholas Park, Jubilee Road, Gosforth, Newcastle-upon-Tyne, NE3 3XT

Typeset and design by Solstice Heritage.

Printed and bound by Jeremy Mills Publishing Limited, 113 Lidget Street, Lindley, Huddersfield, West Yorkshire, HD3 3JR, United Kingdom.

ISBN 978-0-9930789-0-3

Front Cover: Looking out to sea from Low Hauxley.

Rear Cover: View across the excavation trench showing the Beaker-period cairn and the encroaching North Sea beyond.

This book is dedicated to Chris Tolan-Smith who inspired my interest in the Mesolithic.

FOREWORD

When Northumberland Wildlife Trust was first approached by Clive Waddington to become involved in a major archaeological project on the Northumberland coast, adjacent to our Hauxley nature reserve on Druridge Bay, we had to think long and hard about it. Whilst taken up by Clive's enthusiasm and message of rescuing this important site from the ravages of the North Sea, as an organisation, we had never undertaken an archaeological project before and it seemed less than a priority in the bigger scheme of things, for where was the wildlife connection?

Soon however, we became excited by what it might reveal and teach us about the whole environment, cultural and natural, of Druridge Bay and the Northumberland coast. Peat beds exposed on the beach with animal and human footprints, preserved for thousands of years, hinted at the potential to take a long view of the changing human relationship with the Northumberland coast and its ecology over time. As a coastline Druridge Bay is both a dynamic and living landscape and one where humans and nature have interacted over time to create the landscape we enjoy today. Therefore, we resolved to work together to take this vision forward.

This book tells the full story from that point onwards, but it also informs on all the attempts over previous years to get to grips with this important place, where many had seen treasures revealed as the cliff face eroded away. It is remarkable that so much of an archaeological record is held in this one location, hidden under the dunes.

Once up and running, the excavation generated huge interest from volunteers, local people, specialists, the local and national media and visitors, all intrigued by the sequence being revealed day by day in the hot sun of an exceptional summer. We are all indebted to everyone who contributed to help make the project possible, especially The Heritage Lottery Fund (HLF) for its significant financial support, Northumberland County Council and Clive Waddington and his team of experts for carrying out the work. It is certainly one of the best and most exciting projects the Trust has ever been involved in.

Rescued from the Sea did exactly what we hoped it would - shine a light on the landscape of this part of the Northumberland coast, from prehistory to the present. And the story goes on…discoveries continue to be made and the human impact also carries on through the effects of climate change which has, even throughout the past, had a profound effect on people's lives here. If any message is taken away from 'Rescued from the Sea' it is the need to build more resilience into the future for, as it also shows, we are very much a part of nature and subject to the vagaries of natural forces.

This, then, is a story of how people, landscape, ecology and wildlife have adapted together through time, revealed by an amazing archaeological and sediment sequence.

Mike Pratt

CEO Northumberland Wildlife Trust

CONTENTS

LIST OF FIGURES

1. New Discoveries

2. Ice, Sea and Sand

3. The Tide Waits For No Man

4. Dig Deep and All is Revealed

5. Making Sense of Things

6. A Community Strides Forth

7. Loose Ends

PREFACE

This short book describes a remarkable archaeological site and the story of how it was investigated prior to destruction by the North Sea. We live in a time of rapidly rising sea levels and we can observe the profound effects this is having on populations throughout the world today by switching on our televisions, PCs and tablets. The harrowing images that come to mind at the mention of Banda Aceh (Indonesia, December 2004), Hurricane Katrina (USA, August 2005), Fukushima (Japan, March 2011) or Hurricane Sandy (USA, October 2012) serve as a reminder of the catastrophic events that are affecting coastlines throughout the world. The British Isles, although not yet subject to such an extreme event in recent times, are nonetheless subject to rising sea levels and a concomitant increase in coastal erosion. As the cliffs collapse and people's homes, businesses and agricultural land is lost, the destruction of archaeological and palaeoenvironmental remains is also taking place. On every tide archaeological remains somewhere on the British coastline are punished by the relentless impact of the sea and this daily loss of information is one of the key challenges archaeologists are faced with, and will continue to be faced with, for generations to come. In the following chapters I have set out to provide a first-hand account of the excavations undertaken at Low Hauxley in advance of further erosion by the sea, and to share my experiences of this endeavour, in what I hope is an engaging account, with the reader.

To ensure a flowing read I have not employed referencing although a list of suggested reading is provided at the back. The dates referred to throughout the book are expressed as true calendar years BC and AD and should not, therefore, be confused with uncalibrated radiocarbon dates which are not the same. The only exception is the sea level curve in Figure 23 which is expressed in thousands of years before present (ky Bp).

Accompanying this book is a further volume that documents in detail the archaeological results of this study. It has been written in the traditional academic style and examines the themes outlined here in considerably more depth. Further information is also available on the project web pages (www.nwt.org.uk/rescued-from-the-sea) which includes downloadable documents, video clips and links to resources for schools. All the finds from this project have been deposited with the Great North Museum, Newcastle upon Tyne, where selected artefacts are on display with accompanying information. A Channel 4 Time Team documentary that focused on the Bronze Age burials on the site was broadcast in March 2014 and this can be seen on the catch up channels via the internet. The programme was titled 'Britain's Bronze Age Mummies'.

Clive Waddington

September 2014

ACKNOWLEDGEMENTS

This book arose from a project, 'Rescued from the Sea', that sought to record a site with important archaeological remains eroding from a cliff face in Northumberland. The project took years in planning but was quickly executed and none of this would have been possible without the help and input from an epic cast. With over 700 people actively involved in the excavation there is not space to thank each person individually for their contribution, but rest assured their input is greatly valued and I hope all those who have taken part in this endeavour have been given cause for satisfaction and are able to look back at what they have helped to achieve.

There are some individuals, though, who I must single out for their particular help, so in no particular order I would like to acknowledge the following: Jim Nesbitt for his unflagging work in monitoring the site in recent years and being so generous with information and help, and to John Davies who has also kept an eye on the site over the last 30 years, assisted with our excavation and was a member of the 1983 excavation team. The team of professional staff deserve a special mention including, in particular, Philippa Cockburn who has worked tirelessly with me to deliver the 'Rescued from the Sea' project, Jim Brightman for his unflagging dependability as my second in command throughout the excavation and to Kristian Pedersen who helped supervise the excavation and undertook a prodigious job in cataloguing and analysing the flint assemblage. The supreme efforts of other individuals who helped supervise the excavation include Chris Fowler, Kate Mapplethorpe, Laura Strafford, Joe Tong, Dave Cockcroft, Sophie Moore and Lucy Cummings.

Our partners in this project, the Northumberland Wildlife Trust, have supported and managed the project throughout and particular thanks are due to Mike Pratt and Steve Lowe who not only helped with the excavation but also helped direct the project behind the scenes, and who have given support and guidance throughout. Other staff from the Trust who have been of much help throughout include Louise Chapman, Fiona Dryden, Tracy Evans, Lynette Friend, Alex Lister, Elaine More, Joanne Marwood and Laura Lowther. Jacqui Huntley from English Heritage has been typically supportive and I have benefited from her expertise throughout, including in the planning stages. Previous excavators of the site have been very generous with sharing information and advice and in particular I'd like to record my thanks to Steve Speak and Bill Griffiths (formerly of Tyne and Wear Museums Service), Clive Bonsall (Edinburgh University) and to staff at Oxford Archaeology (formerly the Lancaster University Archaeological Unit). Steve and Bill have been particularly helpful and generous with their time and use of their photographs and have offered nothing but encouragement and help throughout and I am indebted to them for this assistance. Clive Bonsall kindly made available information in advance of the excavation and discussed the site in detail with me on a site visit prior to our excavation.

There has been a host of specialist scientists who have assisted throughout this project providing valuable analysis and data and it is a pleasure to acknowledge the important contributions of Jim Innes, Ian Bailiff, Mike Bamforth, Paul Bidwell, Ian Boomer, Tony Brown, Val de Feu, Chris Fowler, Milena Gryzbowska, Sheila Hamilton-Dyer, Jim Innes, Tim Kinnaird, Michael Lobb, Kate Mapplethorpe, Peter Marshall, Andrew Millard, David Sanderson, Ian Shennan, Alison Sheridan, Laura Strafford, Maisie Taylor and Richard Tipping. I would also like to record my thanks to Sara Rushton and Mike Jeffries from Northumberland County Council, Graham Mitcheson from Druridge Bay Country Park and Northumberland County Council and Katie Coombes from Natural England.

I would also like to record the debt of thanks owed to our funders: the Heritage Lottery Fund, English Heritage, UK Coal and the Northumberland Coast and Lowlands Leader Fund without whose help this work could never have taken place. In this regard I must also give a special mention to Steve Scoffin, formerly of the Northumberland Wildlife Trust, who worked closely with me to design the project, make applications for funding and having the vision and confidence to give this initiative a go. Thank you Steve. The project received significant press coverage and featured on various television programmes and it is a pleasure to single out the interest and supportive contributions by Tony Henderson of the Newcastle Journal and Jobim Sampson from Time Team who worked tirelessly with his film crew to produce a documentary based around the excavations on the site, and to the presenters Sir Tony Robinson, Francis Pryor and Phil Harding. The excavation was also captured on film by students of the Hirst Park Middle School Media Crew led by Brian Cosgrove, Web Development and Media Manager with the Ashington Learning Partnership. The professionalism and enthusiasm of the student film-makers made them a real pleasure to work with for all the excavation team. Thanks are also extended to weatherman Ross Hutchinson from Tyne Tees Television who did a sterling job giving weather reports from the site throughout the excavation.

Unless otherwise stated all the images in the book are those of Archaeological Research Services Ltd and for the others I am most grateful to Luc Amkreutz, Nick Best, Vince Gaffney, Great North Museum, Bill Griffiths, National Museum of Antiquities (Netherlands), Jim Nesbitt, Ian Shennan and Steve Speak.

Finally, it is with great fondness I can record my thanks to the entire cast of volunteers who toiled for 13 weeks under the baking Northumberland sun of 2013. Not only did they work hard in sometimes stifling conditions, but they bore it with fortitude, good humour and much camaraderie and it was a delight to have worked with so many wonderful people from all walks of life and with such different and interesting stories. They did a remarkable job and I hope their memories of this shared achievement stay close companions for years to come.

GLOSSARY OF TERMS

Antler mattock	An excavation or pounding tool made from deer antler usually with a hole perforated in it to take a wooden handle.
Baulk	An upstanding wall of in situ sediment, such as a trench edge, on an archaeological excavation.
Batter	The deliberately angled face of an earthen bank made to prevent it from slumping.
Bell pits	Name given to the bell-shaped pits that were excavated in medieval times to extract coal where the bases of the pits flare out and are wider than the shaft.
Climate change proxies	Indirect sources of information that can be used to infer what the climate was like at different times in the past. Typical proxy data include ice cores, tree rings, fossil pollen, boreholes, corals, lake and ocean sediments, and carbonate speleothems.
Composite tool	A form of Stone Age tool that has several functioning parts such as a spear with lots of sharp barbs at its striking end rather than just a single point.
DNA	An acid that carries the genetic information in a cell that can self-replicate. It consists of two chains of nucleotides twisted into a double helix and it is their sequencing that determines individual hereditary characteristics.
Drip gully	Name given to a shallow trench that forms below a roof edge as a result of rainwater running off the roof and dripping to the ground.
Embayment	An indentation of a shoreline forming a bay.
Flotation	A method of sifting archaeological sediment in water so that the light organic fraction floats to the top where it is collected in fine-meshed sieves for analysis.
GPS	'Global Positioning System' that uses satellites to accurately pin-point a location. It is the same technology that is used in vehicle 'sat navs'.
Inhumation	A buried corpse.
Intertidal zone	The area inundated by the sea between the low and high tide marks.
Kerb	Carefully made stone edging.
LGM	Last Glacial Maximum – this is the time when the ice sheets were at their most recent maximum extension, marking the peak of the last glacial period *c*.18,000 BC.
Littoral	A region lying along a shoreline.
Midden	Cooking and food waste such as bone, shell or plant remains.
Palaeoenvironment	A term used to refer to past environments or landscapes.
Palaeosol	An ancient soil, usually buried by later sediments.

Pele tower	Small fortified tower house, common in the Anglo-Scottish Border region, typically dating to the mid 15th to the early 16th centuries.
Radiocarbon date	An age measurement that utilises the time it takes for an isotope of carbon to decay which then provides an age estimate of a given span of years. Radiocarbon dates are not the same as calendar dates and therefore require 'calibrating'.
Relative sea level	This is the averaged level of the sea in relation to land. In the higher latitudes, such as Britain, the tidal range can be very high.
Rock steel	An eroded rock terrace situated in front of a cliff line and extending into the intertidal zone and beyond. A phrase used commonly for such features on the North East British coast.
Sherd	A fragment of something, typically used in reference to pottery fragments in British archaeology.
Site of Special Scientific Interest	Sometimes abbreviated to 'SSSI' this is the name given to designated areas of landscape which have statutory protection on account of their ecological, geological or other environmental significance.
Stratigraphy	Originally a term used in geology, it refers to the stacked layers of sediments, soils and archaeological deposits which lie one on top of the other.
Till	A geolomorphological term used to describe the sediments deposited by glacial action.

1. NEW DISCOVERIES

Ping! Another email landed in my inbox and the message came up to say it was from Jim Nesbitt, a volunteer archaeologist whom I had known for some years and who had worked on one of my earlier excavations at a quarry in north Northumberland. I could see the message had attachments and a faint pulse of excitement crept into me as I wondered whether this could be something interesting that Jim wanted to show me.

Figure 1. Jim Nesbitt, volunteer archaeologist and long-time monitor of the Low Hauxley site.

I opened the email and there were several photographs attached, together with a short message from Jim asking if I wanted to have a look at the site where Jim had photographed some archaeological remains. I immediately opened the first photograph and I could see the white crusty material suggestive of ancient sea shell or burnt bone situated in an exposed cliff face several metres below today's ground surface. The next photograph intrigued me even more as I could make out dry sandstone walling defining what looked to be a circular, or slumped rectangular, building in a different part of the cliff face buried below several metres of sand dune. If these weren't perplexing enough the next photograph showed a series of what appeared to be rectangular pits cut into the bedrock on the foreshore, the photograph obviously having been taken when the tide was out. What on earth were these features? I had not seen rock-cut pits like this before, and certainly not so many all together. It turned out these were the warm-up act because the final photograph showed a small stone box in the cliff face with flecks of white material around its edge. Could this be a cremation burial from millennia past? My interest piqued, I did not bother typing a reply, this required reaching for the telephone.

Jim is a very amiable man with a wonderful Northumbrian accent and a patient demeanour. It was April 2009 and he described to me in accurate detail the discoveries he had made pictured in the photographs, and explained that he had been keeping his eye on this stretch of coastline for the last few years, living only a few miles away. The site was located at the north end of Druridge Bay on the Northumberland coast about half a mile south of the hamlet of Low Hauxley. Archaeological remains have been recorded at this site for over 30 years but what Jim had noticed were new features. After discussing with Jim on the telephone I arranged to meet him on site so we could examine these features together.

The site at Low Hauxley was not new to me as I had been directing a rapid survey of England's North East coast for English Heritage at the time of Jim's email. The purpose of this project was to create an accurate digital map showing where all known archaeological sites were located in the coastal strip in an area extending from Whitby in North Yorkshire to the Anglo-Scottish border north of Berwick-upon-Tweed. Each site was visited on the ground and an assessment was made of its condition, its archaeological importance and the extent to which it was under threat from coastal erosion. We scored each site against a set of criteria to produce a list with the highest priority sites ranked at the top and the least threatened sites at the bottom. The site that had come out at the top of this study was the site at Low Hauxley, but the remains Jim had discovered were new features that had not previously been recorded.

When I arrived at our rendezvous point Jim was already there and we walked from our vehicles along the beach to the site. The first feature we came to was a rock cut pit on the foreshore, but it became instantly apparent that it was only one of several dozen of these features. The pits were typically two or three metres long and one and a half metres wide. The tide had filled all of these pits with beach cobbles and so it was not clear how deep they were, what their internal shape was like and whether any archaeological remains survived in them. These were certainly unusual and our best guess at the time was that they may have been associated with salt production. The remains of a wooden post could be observed in the corner of one of them and there was some rusty iron in another but this could just have been material washed in by the sea. We had made our visit early in the year when winter storms routinely batter this area of coastline and this had meant that the sand cover on the foreshore had been scoured off exposing the rock cut pits. I concluded that the only way to establish what these pits were was by excavating one of them in the hope of finding some clue as to their original function. As it turned out, they were to have served a wholly different purpose and one that we had not suspected.

The next feature we visited was the site of the drystone walled building. This entire feature had been washed away by the sea by the time we got to the site but Jim was able to show me its precise location in the cliff face where it had been situated on top of a conspicuous band of black peat, but buried by several metres of dune sand which had accumulated above it. This band of black peat was very important as it represented the infilling of what had once been a wetland or 'mere'. With it having been waterlogged in the past, organic material survived well and ancient timbers could be observed at the base of this layer a few hundred yards further up the coast. Trapped within the peat were tiny grains of pollen that had been produced by plants and trees in the past and this meant that a record of the past environment was preserved in this sediment. Some years before Jim Innes and Budd Frank from Newcastle and Durham Universities

Figure 2. Placed bone and shell material preserved eroding from the cliff face (© Jim Nesbitt).

Figure 3. Stone-founded building eroding from the cliff face (© Jim Nesbitt).

Figure 4. Rectangular rock-cut pits on the foreshore filled with beach cobble material (© Jim Nesbitt).

Figure 5. Small, par
destroyed, burial ci
eroding from below
the stone cairn in th
cliff face.

respectively and Richard Tipping and Clive Bonsall from Stirling University and Edinburgh University respectively had sampled this peat and studied the pollen profile. As part of this work they had obtained some radiocarbon dates on the sediment sequence and it showed that the top of the peat dated to the centuries around the beginning of the first millennium BC, sometime around 800 BC or thereabouts, and it was after this time that the sand started to accumulate. The stone-walled structure that Jim Nesbitt had photographed lay directly on top of the peat and so must date to sometime shortly after 800 BC but before the sand had started to bury it. This meant the building was probably of considerable antiquity. The shape of the building and the method of dry stone wall construction suggest this had been a small stone-founded building, although Jim's photographs showed that the wall had slumped under the weight of the overlying sand giving it an irregular appearance. This was quite a stunning discovery and I was gutted that the building had been destroyed by the sea with only Jim's photographs as a record of it. Given that the building had been covered by sand the preservation of this structure would have been exceptional. The sand on this stretch of coast is calcareous (ie. contains calcium carbonate) in origin, being made up in part of the crushed fragments of marine shell. This reduces the acidity of the sand and creates a benign environment for the preservation of ancient organic material such as bone. The loss of this site was an opportunity gone begging and as there have been hardly any Late Bronze Age–Early Iron Age houses excavated in this region this structure would have helped to plug a gap in our knowledge. On a subsequent visit, after Jim and myself had inspected the site, Jim discovered a shaped timber, probably some sort of peg, that had been driven into the peat just beyond where the wall of the building had been and could have been part of an associated feature. I took a sample of wood from the peg and sent it away to be radiocarbon dated and the result came back showing the timber dated to the period between 800 and 540 BC. This was consistent with the date the previous investigation of the peat had obtained and shows that the stone-founded building and associated peg were in use around the Late Bronze Age–Early Iron Age prior to its burial by the windblown sand.

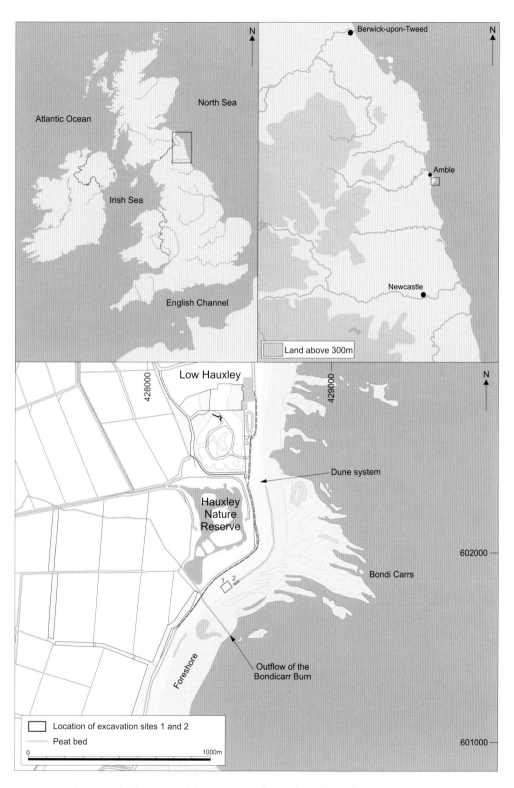

Figure 6. Map showing the location of the Low Hauxley archaeological sites. Site 1 is the location of the large-scale 2013 excavation and Site 2 is the location of the stone-founded building removed by the sea and the 2014 cliff-edge excavation of the Neolithic hearth.

We walked a few yards south to where the stone-lined box was situated in the cliff face. We both knew that 'Beaker' period (c.2400–1800 BC) burials had been recorded eroding out of this bit of cliff face before and we were excited at the prospect of examining this small box-type feature. As we looked at it in closer detail we could see white flecks of burnt bone in the cavity of the box and around its edges indicating this was a small burial chamber for a cremation. These boxes are known as 'cists' (pronounced 'kist') and are typical on Beaker period burial sites in northern England and Scotland.

When Jim had first found the cist he had noticed some white bone-like material at the foot of the cliff in front of the box and it looked as if someone else had got to the feature first and emptied most of the contents out of it. Normally these cremations are found inside finely made pottery jars known as 'Food Vessels' that are frequently placed upside down in the cist. We remain of the opinion that just such a pot had been removed from this cist and some of the bone had fallen out of it when it was pulled out leaving the little pile of burnt material at the foot of the cliff.

We walked on a few more yards studying the cliff face in detail and found the outline, in section, of a pit that had been cut down into the sediments from the top of an ancient land surface which had been subsequently buried by the sand dunes. Again we could see flecks of what appeared to be burnt bone and ash in the fill of this pit together with chipped flints. Immediately overlying both of these features was a pile of rocks indicating that a substantial pile of stones, typically referred to as a cairn, had once covered these features. There was an urgent need to record both of these finds otherwise a few more high tides would soon have them washed away. I made up my mind there and

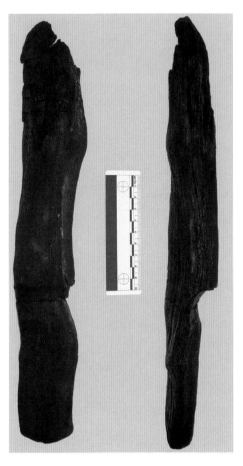

Figure 7. The shape timber 'peg' found by Jim Nesbitt drive in to the top of the cliff-face peat next to the stone-founder building (scale = 10cm).

then that, subject to permission, we had to mount a small excavation to record these remains otherwise they would be lost for good.

This left the patch of white crusty material that Jim had photographed in the cliff face. We searched for it but this, like the stone building, had gone as a result of further erosion of the cliff face. This trip had really brought home to me the importance of a rapid response when archaeological features are noticed eroding out of cliff faces. Depending on the weather conditions they could have hours, days or sometimes a few months before they are removed by the sea, otherwise material would continue to be lost without further record. Looking at the photograph in detail it was not clear whether the white crusty material was the remains of shellfish from a man-made shell midden or the burnt bone of

Figure 8. Eroding pit containing burnt remains exposed in the cliff face below the stone cairn.

another human burial. There was no sign of a pit in the photograph, which is what we would have expected if it had been a burial, but rather the material appeared to be sitting directly on top of the glacial till that had been laid down at the end of the last Ice Age some 18,000 years ago. It was therefore possible that this could be a mound of burnt food remains piled up by some of the first humans to inhabit northern Britain, but unfortunately this is something that cannot now be tested.

The first excavation in the area of the burials took place in February 1983 when Steve Speak, a professional archaeologist, was called in to record a Beaker period burial that had been noticed eroding out of the cliff face. Steve encountered a remarkable scene where a large stone-built cist could be seen perched in the cliff face where it had been exposed after stormy weather. On removing one of the slabs and peering inside Steve could see a remarkably well-preserved human skeleton (an unburnt human burial like this is also referred to as an 'inhumation'). The skeleton had been placed in a crouched, or 'foetal', position lying on its right hand side with the head to the south and the face turned eastwards looking out to sea. Clive Bonsall, an archaeologist from Edinburgh University who was studying the site, visited the burial site shortly afterwards and found a flint

knife associated with the burial and fragments from a decorated pottery vessel made in a distinctive style were also found above this grave, but this was a secondary deposit that was thought to have been dug down to the top of the cist's capstone. It is the commonly held view of archaeologists that these vessels were buried with individuals to provide them with food or drink that would help them on their journey in the afterlife – hence the name 'Food Vessels'.

Later in the same year Clive Bonsall excavated a trench set back from the cliff face through the top of the sand dunes all the way down through the archaeological layers and glacial sediments to the underlying sandstone bedrock. At the seaward end of the excavation trench he found the stone kerb of the large burial cairn that was the same cairn we could see in the cliff face covering Jim's cremation burial and the same one that had covered the burial excavated by Steve. At the other end of the trench he found a separate small cairn. He fully excavated the small cairn and found the skeleton of a young man below it which had been placed directly on the ground surface before the stones of the cairn were piled on top of him. There were no accompanying 'grave goods' with this burial and when it was radiocarbon dated it was found to be a few centuries later in date than the burial

Figure 9. The first burial cist to be noticed eroding from the cliff face at Low Hauxley in 1983 (© Steve Speak).

excavated by Steve, indicating that the small cairn was built later than the first phase of the large cairn. In addition to the burial a substantial number of chipped flints were also found in the ancient ground surface bearing witness to occupation on the site by Mesolithic hunter-gatherer-fishermen. This activity is much older than the Beaker period and hinted at the presence of a more extensive Stone Age site here. With little material available to date the Mesolithic activity the date of this flint scatter could only be ascribed to the roughly 6000 year span that archaeologists call the Mesolithic (which means 'middle Stone Age'). Flint tools are chipped in distinctive styles depending on which period they belong to and this is how it was able to be determined that the flint scatter represented Mesolithic activity. One of the defining characteristics of the Mesolithic stone tool kit is the presence of 'microliths' (meaning 'small stone tool') which are small armatures or barbs that were fastened to arrows, spears, threshing boards and the like to form what archaeologists refer to as 'composite tools'. The type of microliths that were present in the scatter consisted of 'narrow blade' microliths and these

have traditionally been thought to date to the second half of the Mesolithic.

Ten years later, in 1993, high tides and storms tore away more of the cliff and revealed another large stone cist perched in the cliff face below the large stone cairn just a few metres from where Steve Speak had excavated the first cist. A member of the public discovered the cist and informed Northumberland County

Figure 10. John Davies in the blue jumper, a well-known amateur archaeologist, who monitored the Low Hauxley site during the 1980s and assisted with the 1983 and 2013 excavations.

gure 11. The 1983
:cavation led by
ive Bonsall (second
om left) which
nearthed a second,
nall cairn overlying
single burial (at rear
the trench) and the
icient land surface
entre) containing
esolithic flints (©
eve Speak).

Council. This time it was Steve and his colleague Bill Griffiths, from Tyne and Wear Museums Service, who came to the rescue. On this occasion two cists were found built almost back to back, one of which contained the cremated remains of an adult individual and the other a skeleton of another individual. Each burial was accompanied by a finely made Beaker, the cremation having one with a short neck and the inhumation having one with a slightly longer neck. Expert examination of the bones revealed the inhumation burial was probably that of a young man, probably in his late teens, who had a bad abscess in his mouth and who had experienced a period of malnutrition in his earlier life.

I retrieved these remains during 2013 from where they had been kept in storage since 1993 by Northumberland

gure 12. Burial cist
scovered eroding
om the cliff face
1993 (© Bill
·iffiths).

County Council and submitted a sample for radiocarbon dating. The result was quite exciting as it dated the individual to the period 2400–2200 BC, which is a very early date for a Beaker burial in Britain suggesting this was one of the first 'Beaker people' in the region.

By 1993 the importance of this site and the precarious state of the archaeological remains had become apparent. In 1994, English Heritage, in a bid to understand the wider context of the site, commissioned the then Lancaster University Archaeological Unit to undertake two evaluation trench excavations to the rear of the cliff edge burial site and to examine the black peat to the north where Jim Nesbitt was to later discover the stone building. The narrow trenches produced some more Mesolithic flints but the main achievement was establishing that the burial site occupied a small, low hillock and that by the Neolithic and Bronze Age the lower ground around it had become a wetland leaving the hillock as more or less an 'island' standing proud of a marsh, or 'mere', that would have been set back behind a dune system further out to sea than the current dunes.

Between 1994 and the recent work described below, no further work was undertaken. One of the key problems that the site had always faced was that because it wasn't being damaged by development or any other man-made threat there wasn't a mechanism in place to deal with such a site and no one organisation had responsibility for it. This is a serious problem with much of our nation's eroding coastal archaeology as these sites tend to fall betwixt and between. Consequently, many of them continue to be eroded without any record as there is no nationally appointed system in place to deal with these types of sites.

As I stared at the crumbling remains in the cliff face with Jim I realised that

Figure 13. The human burial and Beaker pot from the first cist excavated in 1993 (© Bill Griffiths).

excavating the small cist and pit was just a holding measure and that if any sense was ever going to be made of this remarkable group of sites, as it was clear now there was far more here than a Beaker period burial cairn and Mesolithic flints, then a much bigger project was needed that would rescue this site once and for all. I knew this was not going to be easy because not only was the UK in a deep recession but the funding priorities of organisations such as English Heritage were also changing. One way or another I'd find a way of getting this work done but I'd have to do some serious legwork to bring stakeholders on board as a project of the scale I had in mind would need a broad base of support if it was ever going to take place.

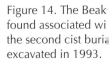

Figure 14. The Beaker found associated with the second cist burial excavated in 1993.

2. ICE, SEA AND SAND

Coastlines, particularly in the higher latitudes, tend to be highly dynamic environments where erosion and deposition of sediments occur with regular frequency, occasioned by the relentless daily tides as well as rarer, but highly destructive, storm events. On the eastern side of Britain the ever-changing coastal environment has a particularly colourful history having only come into being as a coastline in the recent geological past. Looking out on to the North Sea from the cliffs at Low Hauxley it is not always easy to appreciate that our first ancestors who walked this land would have looked out over a different scene comprising dry land for many miles towards a distant embayment beyond. In short, much of what is now the North Sea was once dry land and Britain was connected to the Continent by a large expanse of land that now lies submerged below the sea. To understand this remarkable story of how Britain became an island and how our coastline was formed we have to look back to the Ice Age.

Around 15,000 BC global temperatures started to rise dramatically bringing the last glacial maximum (often referred to as the LGM for short) to a close. The melting ice sheets discharged huge amounts of water into the world's seas giving rise to inexorable sea level rise. At the same time some of the land that had been covered by ice, relieved of this huge weight, started to bounce back up. This had a see-saw effect though, which meant that lower lying ice-free land on the other side of the 'hinge' that had previously been tilted up started to sink. These are complex processes and there is much localised variability but the overall picture is that the north and west of Britain has been generally rising ever since whilst the south and east have been falling. This last phase of the Pleistocene, or Ice Age, is known by archaeologists as the Late Upper Palaeolithic.

The gradual warming after the LGM was not, however, continuous. It was punctuated by a severe downturn in temperature that instigated another glacial period known as the Younger Dryas across North West Europe, or the Loch Lomond Stadial in Britain, between c.11,000 and 9700 BC. During this period the human populations that had colonised the British Isles and North Sea Plain may have stayed in the southern parts of this region but the archaeological evidence for continued occupation is slim, so that even if human groups did stay it would have been in relatively small numbers. The geneticist Stephen Oppenheimer argues for a continued human presence through this cold snap on the basis that he sees no evidence of genetic alterations or interruption at this time, but ultimately this is highly

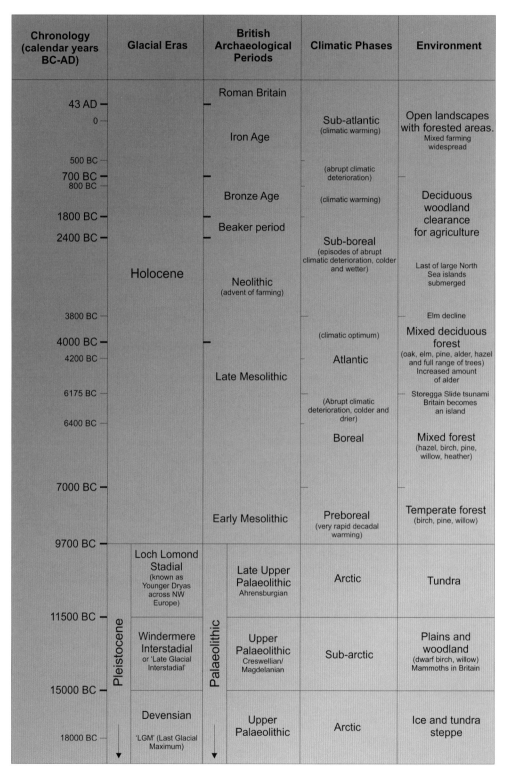

Figure 15. Time chart showing archaeological periods alongside geological, climatic and environmental phases.

interpretive as the age estimates for DNA mutations are unknown and other explanations could account for the genetic pattern he has observed. Still, it remains possible that human occupation continued in the southern part of what is now the British Isles. The Loch Lomond Stadial came to an abrupt end around 9700 BC when temperatures rose once again, but this time more quickly than after the LGM, heralding the geological period known as the Holocene. Within perhaps less than a century the land in the north had become habitable and the recolonisation by an increasingly rich flora and fauna meant there were rich lands once again for hunter, gatherer and fishing groups. This climatic change heralded the period archaeologists refer to as the Mesolithic, which coincides with the early Holocene, and it accounts for one of the most exciting periods in our history when Britain became fully colonised by human groups, the landscape underwent dramatic change from polar conditions to verdant forest, the North Sea Plain was drowned and Ireland, followed by Britain, became islands. The temperatures became so clement that the centuries between *c.*6500 and 3500 BC are known as the 'climatic optimum' because annual summer temperatures were around 2° centigrade higher than they are today, making the landscape more productive and giving rise to a wider variation of plants and animals. This, however, should not be thought of as a uniform climate because, as we know today climate can vary considerably within a given time period, so that for example we now know that there were five cold snaps or 'neo-glacials' during the Mesolithic period in Europe which gave rise to significant environmental events and these will have affected human population numbers and subsistence strategies.

The North Sea is young, having only separated Britain off from the Continent

around 6200 BC as sea level rose. It is also very shallow, although there are occasional deep trenches where ancient estuaries have scoured more deeply into the underlying bedrock, such as the linear trench known as the 'Outer Silver Pit'. Modern sea level is only 15–30 metres above the Dogger Bank, whilst around the Danish littoral sea level can be as shallow as just one or two metres above the sea floor over large tracts of the in-shore waters. The North Sea, particularly around the British coastline, is also remarkable for its huge tidal ranges which can reach over 14 metres around the Bristol Channel and the Channel Islands. In fact the Bristol Channel has the second highest tidal reach anywhere in the world.

Prior to the breaching of the last swathe of land connecting Britain to mainland Europe there was an embayment to the north that extended southwards between what is today Scotland and Norway, whilst to the south there were two embayments: one running between Brittany and Normandy and the English south coast and one running between the west British coast and Ireland. At this time Ireland was connected to Britain via a small land bridge between Antrim and the Argyll coast. The rivers Ouse, Humber, Elbe and Weser, Ems and Scheldt all flowed into the North Sea embayment, whilst rivers such as the Thames, Rhine and Seine flowed southwards and fed the embayment that was to become the English Channel. By *c.*9000 BC, if not before, the rising sea had breached the land bridge between Antrim and Argyll separating Ireland from the rest of Britain. As waters rose in the North Sea Basin the low lying areas of the North Sea Plain became sensitive to slight changes in sea level and the effects of storm events. Around 6200 BC there was a cold snap, frequently referred to as the '8.2 kyr event' (referring to 8200 years before the present, rather than BC) and this

Figure 16. Schematic map of Britain *c.*10,000 BC (derived from various sea level models including Coles 1998).

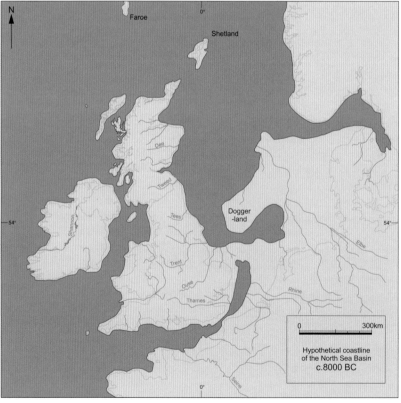

Figure 17. Schematic map of Britain *c.*8000 BC (derived from various sea level models including Sturt *et al.* 2013).

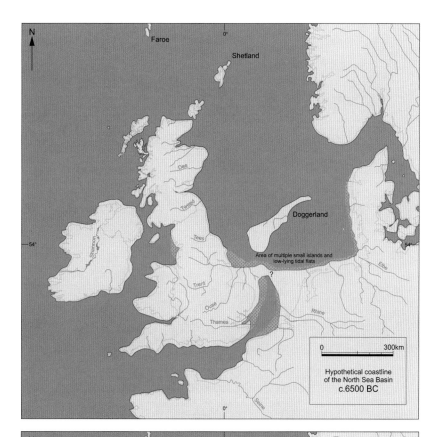

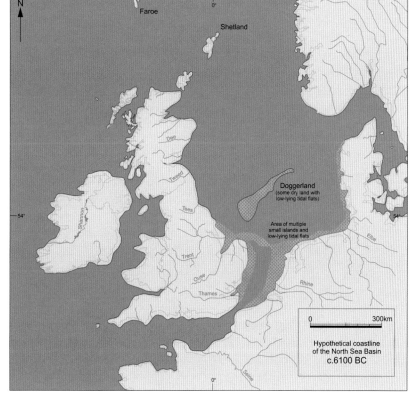

Figure 20. Mesolithi bone points dredgee from the Brown Bank, North Sea (© National Museum c Antiquities, Leiden, the Netherlands).

precipitated a catastrophic underwater rock collapse in the Norwegian Trench that sent a violent, huge tsunami, or tidal surge, into the Atlantic and North Sea embayment. This event is typically referred to as the 'Storegga Slide' and evidence for this in the form of marine sediment spreads has been found along the North East British coast, including as far south as Howick, in Northumberland, where Ian Boomer and I had discovered evidence for this very powerful tidal surge in 2002. I speculated that this storm surge event could have been the one that breached the remaining area of land connecting Britain with North West Europe thus making Britain into an island. After discussing this with a German colleague, Bernhard Weninger, at a conference meeting in Brussels he subsequently published a further case for this interpretation, but it should be cautioned that there is still insufficient evidence to be sure that it was the Storegga tsunami that finally granted Britain its island status, although on balance this is the most likely scenario. It

is only in recent decades that the Storegga Slide and the resultant tsunami has been recognised and there is a growing wealth of scientific study being undertaken in relation to this catastrophic event. Consequently both earth scientists and archaeologists are only just beginning to get to grips with the full implications of this event, although to put it into a wider context, Jon Hill from Imperial College has modelled the size of wave that would have been created based on the volume of rock known to have collapsed into the Norwegian Trench, and this has allowed him to conclude that the volume of the Storegga Slide was around 300 times the global discharge of all rivers to the oceans and it dwarfed the largest slide yet found on land. To say that the Storegga Slide tsunami was catastrophic is perhaps an understatement; it not only changed the geography of Atlantic North West Europe, Britain, the North Sea islands, Ireland and what was to become the Baltic, but it must have had a correspondingly terrifying, calamitous and damaging effect on the human

Figure 21. (left)
Selection of Late
Pleistocene–Early
Holocene animal
bones dredged
from the North Sea
(© Luc Amkreutz,
National Museum of
Antiquities, Leiden,
the Netherlands).

Figure 22. (right)
Two Neolithic
'Michelsburg
Culture' axe heads
both dredged from
the Brown Bank,
North Sea, dating
within the period
4200–3000 BC (©
National Museum of
Antiquities, Leiden,
the Netherlands).

populations occupying these coastlines.

In 1931 a trawler dredged up a carved bone point, probably one of the prongs from a fish spear, from the Leman and Ower Bank off the East Anglian coast revealing for the first time evidence that people had once lived on the land underneath what is now the southern North Sea. Since then over a hundred of these points have been trawled up from the Brown Bank off the Dutch coast, together with antler mattocks and around 60 tons of animal bones – most of this material can be seen in the National Museum of Antiquities, Leiden, the Netherlands. Around the Danish coast there have been over 2300 marine finds and Mesolithic burials have even been found and excavated in the shallow waters that lap today's Danish shoreline. Most recently a large-scale innovative survey of part of the southern North Sea by Vince Gaffney, Simon Fitch, David Smith and the late Ken Thompson, at Birmingham University, using marine seismic survey has brought this part of the sea bed into stark relief

so that the hills, valleys, river courses, estuaries, marshes and coastal plains of this drowned world can once again be seen and mapped.

As a stone tool specialist I have looked at the entire flint collections of the Great North Museum in Newcastle and those at Sunderland Museum as well as at the many tens of thousands of flints found from fieldwalking and excavation projects in the region. One of the characteristics that I had documented for the flint tool assemblages from North East coastal sites was that they often contained flint tools that had been hand chipped in the past but which had then been rolled and naturally abraded in the sea for many years where they typically acquired a new 'skin', or patina, due to the absorption of water. This is a slow process and is usually thought to take several thousand years. These flints are regularly washed onto the North East coast where they can be picked up today. But at coastal Mesolithic sites such as Howick, which has been accurately radiocarbon dated to around

7900 BC, these early chipped flints were being picked up from the beach and re-chipped into new tools even in 7900 BC. This could only mean that the rolled and patinated chipped flints found on the beach at this time were coming from much earlier eroding Stone Age sites under what is now the North Sea, and that dated to the Late Upper Palaeolithic between 15,000 and 9700 BC, when human groups first colonised what was then the North Sea Plain. These re-worked flints provide yet further testimony to the widespread human settlement of the North Sea Plain, or 'Doggerland' as it has come to be known, thousands of years prior to it becoming drowned by rising sea level.

The implications of all of this evidence are profound as it gives the British Isles a very distinct and complex history not only in terms of how our landscape and littoral formed and changed over a very short period of geological time, but also how our islands became colonised and re-colonised throughout the last 17,000 or so years. At a broad scale we can see how climate and geography have shaped the course of human colonisation in North West Europe through the changing availability of habitable land, temperature extremes and the spread of different types of vegetation, fish and fauna after the last Ice Age.

When Britain became separated from Europe around 6200 BC the geography of the British Isles was yet again transformed. Not only was the land artery severed but several large islands were left marooned in the North Sea. The high ground, today referred to as 'banks', such as the Dogger Bank, Brown Bank, Leman and Ower Bank, Ling Bank and so on, were islands still comprising substantial tracts of dry land within the North Sea and there is evidence emerging that some of them continued to be inhabited, even into the Early Neolithic in the late 5th and early 4th millennia BC. An antler

artefact dredged up from the North Sea floor has been radiocarbon dated to around 4000 BC whilst two ground and polished stone axe heads of the Neolithic Michelsberg Culture have been dredged up from the Brown Bank off the Dutch coast and two Neolithic ground stone axe heads made from volcanic tuff have been dredged from the Dogger Bank and are in the collection of the Craven Museum, Skipton. It would seem that the last of the North Sea islands were drowned sometime in the Early Neolithic perhaps creating a human population displacement that may have encouraged the spread of farming communities into eastern Britain. By 4000 BC the British coastline had achieved more or less the configuration that we are familiar with today, although there have been pulses of rise and fall since, such as the rise of a metre or so above modern mean sea level noted along parts of the central and south Northumberland coastline during the Bronze Age – Early Iron Age.

Many of the changes to our island geography that have occurred since the last Ice Age have left traces in the cliff face sediments at Low Hauxley. In fact the layering of sediments on parts of the Northumberland coast is so impressive that they are protected as 'Sites of Special Scientific Interest'. Taking a stroll along the beach at Low Hauxley one cannot help but notice the huge expanses of black peat perched in the cliff face or the thick layers of sand interspersed with thin darker layers also in the cliff face. These dark layers represent ancient buried soils, often referred to as 'palaeosols', and testify to periods of stability in the past when the underlying sediments had acquired a soil and turf cover. Since the Bronze Age, however, windblown sand has accumulated in a series of distinct episodes above these ancient soils and sediments to build the dune system that exists today. In geomorphological terms the dune system that garlands Druridge Bay has been an 'aggrading' environment, that is, one where sediments have continued to build up. This has resulted in the stunning sequence of sediments that can be seen today which are interspersed with archaeological remains of different periods throughout the profile. Due to the effect of rising sea level the dune system today is an 'eroding' environment which means that the sediments built up over the last 12,000 years are in the process of being cut back and removed by the impact of the sea. Within the next fifty years most of this ancient dune system will have been removed.

Druridge Bay is also of special significance because it is located on the hinge, or tipping point, between North West Britain on one side that is titling upwards and South East Britain on the other side that is tilting downwards, and this adds further to the unique circumstances of the Low Hauxley sediments. What has become clear to me over the years, as a geoarchaeologist, is that to understand any archaeological site it is essential that the geomorphology of a site is established so that the archaeology can be properly interpreted and understood.

If we were going to make sense out of the site at Low Hauxley we were going to have to study the sediment sequence in detail to unravel its intriguing story.

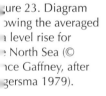

Figure 23. Diagram showing the averaged sea level rise for the North Sea (© Vince Gaffney, after Jelgersma 1979).

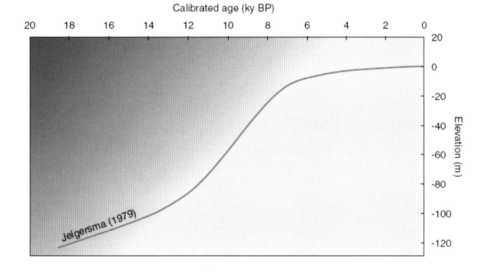

3. *THE TIDE WAITS FOR NO MAN*

After my meeting with Jim Nesbitt on the beach at Low Hauxley I adopted a two-pronged strategy for dealing with the remains. First, I needed to mount a short and effective excavation to record the stone cist and pit eroding from the cliff face below the stone cairn. Secondly, I would have to set up a larger project to excavate a substantial chunk of the site otherwise the problem of annual erosion of remains without record was set to continue. The idea of making a proactive strike for once, in advance of the sea destroying and exposing remains first, seemed a logical approach and one that would give us the initiative rather than having to react to the temperamental whims of nature. This was going to be quite a big ask as funding was getting increasingly hard to come by, given the depth of the recession, and there was a morass of red tape that would have to be navigated through as well. Time was of the essence though, and unless

Figure 24. Excavati[n]g the small burial cis[t] at Low Hauxley in 2009.

we could get a large-scale project in place soon more of the archaeology was going to be lost to the sea without note. The Government's estimates of coastal erosion for this stretch of coastline are in the order of half a metre per year, but I knew from anecdotal evidence that erosion is much more variable than this and can be up to several metres on some parts of this coastline in one year alone and less in others. Sea level is rising at the moment and will continue to do so for many decades, and perhaps centuries, so doing nothing would be to consign these remains to an inexorable fate. Dealing with the most vulnerable remains first we mounted a small rescue excavation of the cist and pit in the cliff face within a few weeks of the initial reconnaissance mission I had made with Jim.

In order for the excavation to go ahead permission was sought from Northumberland County Council as the landowners of the site. On gaining permission myself and a small team set out to record what was left. The day we arrived was incredibly sunny and this

made a change from the bleak windy days which I had become accustomed to on previous visits to the site. I had assembled a small team to undertake the excavation which included Kristian Pedersen and Ben Johnson who had both worked on the Howick site with me in 2000 and 2002. The Howick excavation had been a large-scale investigation of a Mesolithic site on the Northumberland coast. It had produced the first evidence for what was probably a permanent settlement during the Mesolithic in Britain and, as a result, this project had helped to redefine how the Mesolithic was understood. Philippa Cockburn, who had helped with one of the reconstructions of the Howick house, joined Kristian, Ben and myself, together with volunteers Jim Nesbitt and Pat Fenwick who were not going to be missing any of the action. It was June 2009 and stage one was underway.

To access the cist we had to use a ladder as it was situated quite high up in the cliff face – about 1.5 metres above the beach. This meant that only one person could work on excavating the feature from above at any one time. We took it in turns to dig away the overlying sand and then wedged in some wooden boards in front of the sand face so as to hold it back for long enough while we excavated the compact stone cist. There was a shallow cover of stone rubble from the overlying cairn above the small cist box, together with some red ochre. After cleaning with a trowel and brush the stones were photographed and drawn before removal. When this capping was lifted away the carefully made stone-lined box was revealed together with small fragments of burnt human bone around its edges. These were carefully collected and bagged ready for our bone specialist to have a look at them back in the office. There were a few quite large pieces of bone so I knew at least some of the fragments could be identified and there seemed to be enough bone sufficiently well-preserved to allow for a radiocarbon date to be obtained on it.

This was a promising start. Once the stone burial box had been fully explored it was drawn and photographed and a written description of it was made. This is the standard method for recording archaeological features and we were in a hurry as the cliff was unstable and we didn't want to take any longer than was necessary to record what was left of this burial structure.

The next day we returned and our attention focused on the pit. We cut back a small section of the overlying sediment and Jim and Pat cleaned this back to expose the top of the pit. Philippa carefully excavated the fill of the pit using a trowel and a plasterer's leaf and her careful work was rewarded by finding not only the fragmentary remains of another human cremation, but also the

fragments of a burnt pottery vessel that had collapsed under the weight of the material pressing down on it, and which appeared to have originally contained the cremation, together with a few dozen chipped flints which must have been from an earlier period given the style in which they had been chipped. I had been looking very carefully at the sediment sequence in the cliffs and could identify a very ancient buried soil, or palaeosol, and this soil contained Mesolithic flints which could be picked out from the cliff face. It was flints of this much earlier period that were found in the pit fill with the cremation burial. The pit for this cremation burial had been cut through this ancient soil and so the flints must have fallen in when the pit was backfilled with the soil and this had resulted in the mixing of these more ancient artefacts with the burial deposit. Again there was sufficient bone that looked well enough preserved to obtain a radiocarbon date, so this was looking to be a worthwhile operation. We recorded the cremation pit and accurately surveyed the location of the features, then packed up and left the site.

When I got back to the office I rang English Heritage to see if they would be able to run some radiocarbon dates for us on the human bone as part of the rapid coastal zone assessment that we were undertaking at the time. They agreed and samples from each cremation were sent off to the radiocarbon laboratory

Figure 27. The part-eroded pit in the cli face under excavati (left) and the small burial cist under excavation (centre).

Figure 28. The fragmentary remains of a Food Vessel that had contained a human cremation from the cliff face pit.

at Oxford. There is always a palpable air of excitement when radiocarbon dates come back as you can never be quite sure what the result is going to be. In the past I would normally receive a hard copy letter in the post but on this occasion I got the result sent to me via email before I received the posted hard copy. It was with some excitement that I opened the email and there we had it, both of the burials dated to the end of the Beaker period. The cremation from the small cist dated to *c*.2010–1875 BC whilst the cremation from the pit was a little later dating to *c*.1890–1690 BC. This was a great result as it meant we had some data that could be used to help piece together the sequence of the large stone burial cairn under which these burials had been found, but we would need some more dates on the other burials in order to do that. The pottery vessel was an unusual form of Food Vessel and this corresponded well with the dates that we had received.

While I had been on site I took a wander behind the sand dunes to the Northumberland Wildlife Trust's Nature Reserve which occupies the void of an old opencast coal mine. Today it is a peaceful sanctuary for a wide range of bird life and there is a pleasant walk around the pond to the visitor centre and car park. Here I visited a small reconstruction of the stone burial cist that Steve Speak had excavated back in 1983 using the exact stone slabs that had formed the cist. I thought this was a good way of informing the public about what had been discovered as there was no realistic way of having any kind of interpretation on the beach or cliff top, particularly given its susceptibility to erosion. Not long afterwards I met an officer of the Northumberland Wildlife Trust, Steve Scoffin, at a consultation event hosted by Natural England designed to find out what stakeholders thought were the key priorities for the south-east Northumberland coast. I mooted the problems we were faced with at the archaeological site at Low Hauxley and Steve was not only well-informed himself but was also anxious to get something done about it. I visited the Wildlife Trust to discuss with Steve, and also Mike Pratt the Chief Executive, what could be done and we resolved to try and set up a large-scale project to rescue the remains. I thought a partnership approach was the best way to tackle this site as not only were there many different issues around it, but it would also mean we could tap into the experience and knowledge of the Wildlife Trust and the Wildlife Trust could tap into our experience of recording coastal archaeology and running community excavation projects.

Over the following 18 months Steve, Mike and myself gave presentations, attended meetings and consultation events and put in expressions of interest for various grant funds. We sought permissions from the various stakeholders and worked hard to raise the profile of the site so that other key stakeholders understood what was at risk here and the reality of its inevitable destruction. Eventually we got to the point where Steve and I could put pen to paper and start writing the lengthy applications which included plans for community engagement, method statements, costs and a clear timetable.

The applications were submitted and we had to sit tight for several months until the results were determined.

As we were putting the applications together the winter storms in January 2010 scoured an area of foreshore close to the site we had excavated in 2009 and revealed a thin layer of black peat in the intertidal zone on the beach that had never been recorded before. Jim Nesbitt had been down to the site after one of the storms to check if anything had come up and he was amazed at what he saw. He had discovered human and animal footprints preserved all across the top of this peat together with lots of pieces of ancient wood poking out of it. He took some digital photographs and when the email came through to me I was straight on the telephone again to Jim. This was a striking discovery and it would add a whole new dimension to the site. I was aware of the need to record these remains quickly because they would either get washed away by the powerful winter waves or a deposit of beach sand would get dumped on it and we would

Figure 29. Initial recording of the intertidal peat with human and animal footprints visible on its surface.

Figure 30. Human footprints visible on the surface of the intertidal peat.

not be able to get at it again until another storm event scoured the sand off. I made a rapid visit to the site with my long-time colleague David Passmore from the Geography Department at Newcastle University, and Andrew Burn who was mapping this area of coast as part of our rapid coastal survey for English Heritage. When we got to the site and met Jim a storm was in full swing and the tide was on its way in. We were going to have to work fast. Andrew took a series of GPS survey points so we had an accurate record of the patch of surviving peat and its height in relation to sea level, while myself and Dave cleared a few prints out and photographed them. I also took some samples of wood for identification. Within 30 minutes of our arrival the tide

was in and the footprints were buried, but at least we had an initial record.

Over the following days I despatched a team to record the footprints as they remained visible for a few more days. It was not easy work as it had also snowed and the weather was bitterly cold. The team worked hard to empty each footprint of the sand, shingle and ice cold water that filled them, before drawing and photographing them and putting them on to a plan. It was a race against time and just before the recording could be finished the incoming tide dumped a substantial thickness of sand over the peat which buried them again. It was not until after a winter storm in 2012 that the footprints were revealed again. This time, the surviving area was much reduced in size due to large plates of it having been removed by the scouring effect of the sea. The team was despatched again and they completed recording what was left of the peat and the footprints. During the course of this work we collected more wood samples and also took a sample through the peat which could be examined for ancient pollen and plant remains that could be used to date it. We found lots of ancient hazelnut shells

Figure 31. Animal footprint of wild bo on the surface of th intertidal peat.

Figure 32. Cleaning out and recording th hoof and footprints during low tide in 2010.

gure 33. The broken
d deer antler found
the intertidal zone
Low Hauxley
nich may have
ashed out of the
ff-face before being
mped by the tide.

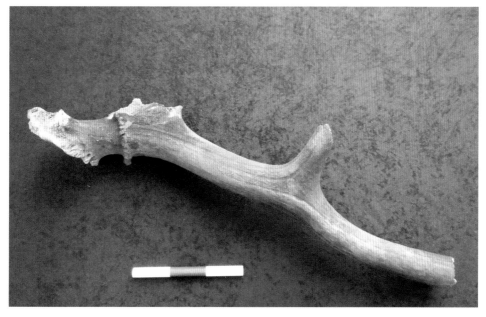

on the surface of the peat and a passer-by alerted us to a red deer antler that he had found on the peat surface. We took a small sample from the deer antler for radiocarbon dating and this returned a Neolithic date of *c.*3000 BC.

The peat had originally built up in a shallow wetland which backed on to a woodland dominated by alder but with occasional elm, oak and hazel amongst others. Our dating of this peat showed that it had started to form in the late Mesolithic around 5400 BC. A few centuries later, around 5100 BC, the peat had become very wet and humans and animals stepped across this marshy ground for the last time leaving their footprints and hoofprints embedded in the peat surface for millennia to come. The peat was rapidly inundated by the sea which 'killed' the peat and the trees and fossilised the footprints below a layer of sand. It was only with the destructive effects of modern sea level rise that the sand has been scoured off again and these footprints and hoofprints were visible for a few fleeting days when we were able to record them before they were washed away.

Finally, in autumn 2012, the responses to our applications were all in and the Wildlife Trust received the news that both of the applications to the Leader Fund and the Heritage Lottery Fund had been successful. Everyone was thrilled as it meant that at last the site could be properly recorded before any more material was lost. It was now a question of timing it right because the winter storms were on their way and there was no prospect of excavating the site in such weather. If we had excavated the cliff face during the winter the trench would have had the tide coming in on most days making excavation pointless. We would have to cross our fingers that the winter storms of 2012–13 would be light and that no great archaeological damage would happen. The excavation was planned for the next window of opportunity which was the summer of 2013. In the event the storms of winter 2012–13 proved fairly subdued which meant that we could plan for the excavation to start in June when hopefully we would get some clement weather.

4. Dig Deep and All is Revealed

The winter of 2012–13 turned out to be mild with an unusually benign impact on the Low Hauxley cliffs. This raised the prospect of us being able to maximise the recovery of archaeological remains when we started to excavate in the early summer. From April 2013 onwards the organisation of staff, contractors and volunteers progressed in earnest and detailed planning went into organising logistics and working through the details of the methodology.

Excavation started on 17th June. The plant contractors, Straughan's of Bedlington, arrived and we discussed how we were going to strip off the turf and topsoil mat and then take the cliff face sediments down in spits to create a rectangular-shaped trench with battered sides and a sloping access track to allow the dumpers to exit the trench and dump the spoil. This work took place under strict archaeological supervision as we were now peeling back thousands of years of history with each bucket scoop. Stuart, the digger driver, performed a remarkable job of carefully excavating back the layers over a large, and increasingly deep, area. Although we knew we had to come down carefully on to the stone cairn we had observed in the cliff face we did not know what else we might encounter as we machined through the various layers of sediment.

Archaeologists have borrowed from geology the concept of 'stratigraphy'; a

Figure 34. Excavation of the site begins by excavating out part the cliff face.

ʒure 35. Excavation
ɔceeds carefully
◢h a tracked
◢cavator under
:haeological
ɔervision.

Figure 35. Excavation proceeds carefully with a tracked excavator under archaeological supervision.

term which is used by archaeologists to describe the building up of successive layers of sediment, soils and man-made deposits. Typically the lowest deposit is the oldest and the highest is the youngest. This logic holds true much of the time unless it is complicated by landforming effects such as landslips, hillwash and so forth which can mix these layers up. At Low Hauxley we had a stunning sequence of intact layers, bedded horizontally, which meant that archaeological remains found in any given layer could be assigned to a specific period and this would be very helpful as we recorded the site. But the problem of excavating deep stratigraphic sites such as this is that excavation takes place back to front, in the sense that it is the last (i.e. youngest) remains that are excavated first and only when they are removed can archaeologists get to the earlier layers. Hence the youngest remains are exposed and recorded first and the oldest remains are exposed and recorded last. And yet it is the early remains and the activity which they represent that often create the circumstances for how and why succeeding phases of activity happen. We, as archaeologists, can only recognise that after we have removed the younger, overlying material which

means we cannot go back to it to look at in the light of what we know from the layers below. In the following sections, therefore, the discoveries from Low Hauxley are described in chronological order from the oldest to the youngest rather than the order in which they were excavated as this provides the most coherent way of understanding how the site developed.

Mesolithic

The Mesolithic is the period of the first Postglacial hunter-gatherers and in Britain this dates from the end of the last Ice Age, c.9700 BC to 4000 BC. At Low Hauxley we discovered an ancient buried soil, or palaeosol, that lay directly above the till laid down by the melting glaciers. Over 15,000 flint tools and chips belonging to this period were found within this soil and we surveyed each one so that we had an accurate plan of where they were found. We also discovered a shallow scoop, about six metres across, which had a very high concentration of flints within it together with a central pit and other traces of internal stone settings. The fill of this scoop also contained charred hazelnut shells and these produced radiocarbon dates which showed it was in use, though

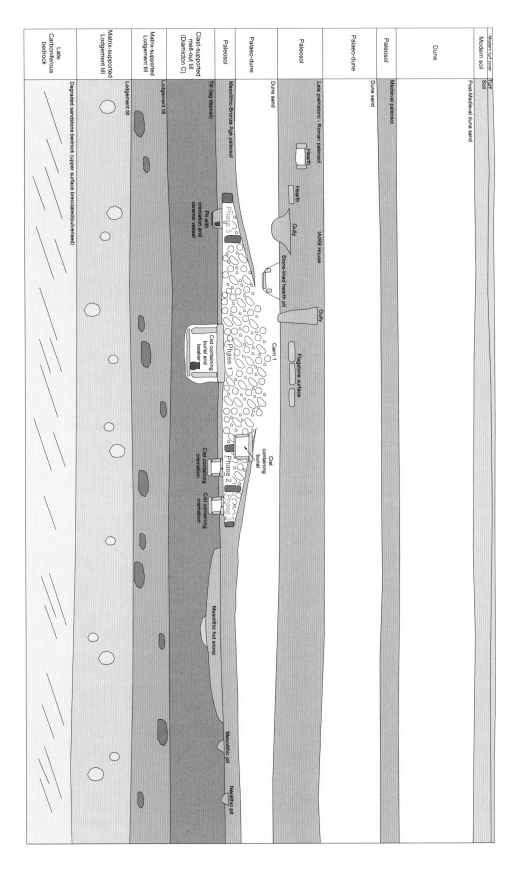

Figure 36. A schematic section of the cliff face showing a stylised section through the full sequence of deposits.

Figure 37. View of the Mesolithic hut 'scoop' with opposite quarters of the circular floor deposits excavated.

probably not continuously, between c.8000 and 7650 BC. This scoop is interpreted as the remnants of a hut-type settlement, probably much like a teepee, which was erected over the scoop time and again by a returning group. Within the structure flint tools had been used to undertake jobs such as scraping and softening animal skins, piercing skins for sewing and they were also shaped into barbs for inclusion in hunting weapons. These small sharp barbs are referred to as 'microliths' by archaeologists and are very distinctive of the Mesolithic period. The presence of hazelnut shells shows that nuts were being collected in the autumn months and consumed on the site whilst the presence of occasional marine shells in the scoop also showed

that shellfish were being collected from the shore. Further evidence for the exploitation of the shore became clear when the flints were examined. Virtually all the flint from this period used on the site had been collected from the beach where it is washed in on a daily basis by the sea. Normally northern regions of Britain, such as Northumberland, are considered to be devoid of flint but this is not the case as beach pebble flint can be found along the entirety of the North East coast. Other artefacts recovered from the hut scoop included some bevelled pebble tools made from sandstone and some small pieces of ochreous material.

Beyond the hut scoop several pits were identified in the buried soil layer

Figure 38. (left) Mesolithic flint 'cores' from which blades have been struck off which would then have been modified into tools.

Figure 39. (right) Mesolithic scalene triangle 'microliths' likely to have been used as barbs for arrows or spearing weapons.

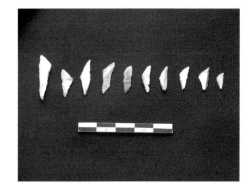

Figure 40. (left) Bevelled pebble rubbing tools.

Figure 41. (right) An excavated Mesolithic pit that produced flints and charred hazelnut shells.

although they were very difficult to observe as the sun dried the soil out so quickly. The summer of 2013 turned out to be one of the driest and sunniest summers for many years, and particularly along the Northumberland coast. This was great for residents and tourists but it made for challenging conditions on the dig as the drying out of the soil meant that the entire surface looked a pale grey or brown, and the colour of the pit fills blurred into the surrounding soil making it difficult to define edges and to even spot the pits. As we got our eyes accustomed to spotting these subtle features several pits were identified and each produced chipped flints and charred hazelnut shells indicating other types of Mesolithic activity beyond the hut area. The radiocarbon dates from these pits show that some were used

when the hut scoop was used but others were made in the centuries afterwards. These dates showed that Mesolithic occupation on the site as a whole took place from at least *c*.7900–7200 BC. This suggests that groups of hunter-gatherer-fishers kept coming back to this site over many generations to hunt and fish and to collect resources from the beach. These people would have been highly adapted to the rhythms of the world, the ebb and flow of the tide and the seasonal availability of different foodstuffs, whether animals, fish or birds.

Neolithic

The Neolithic is the name of the period given to the first farming communities which, in Britain, dates from *c*.4000 to 2400 BC. The evidence for

Figure 42. Wetting the site with water kept the sediments from drying out so that archaeological features remained visible.

gure 43. An Early
eolithic 'leaf-
aped' arrowhead
m the site.

Neolithic activity consisted of several characteristically Neolithic flint tools, such as a fine leaf-shaped arrowhead, a pit from the main excavation site dated by radiocarbon to *c*.3825 BC and a large open air stone hearth that we found in the cliff face a few metres to the north of the main excavation site at Site 2 (see Fig. 6) that was dated to *c*.3600 BC. All this activity falls into the Early Neolithic and therefore represents some of the first farming groups in the region. The presence of the pit and various Neolithic flints is suggestive of settlement activity whilst the presence of the open air hearth, which had burnt wood and Neolithic struck flints around it, was situated in a perennially wet hollow which suggests this was made and used on a seasonal basis, presumably during the dry summer months. The hearth is therefore the result of seasonal activity and implies short expeditions rather than permanent settlement.

These findings are quite significant as there is a lively debate at the moment in British archaeology about whether Neolithic people deliberately avoided coastal resources in favour of terrestrial resources or whether the coast was exploited but we just have not yet been able to pick it up in the archaeological record.

The Low Hauxley evidence points towards coastal exploitation, and perhaps settlement, but on an occasional basis, in this area at least. Unequivocal evidence for permanent coastal settlement remains, however, elusive.

Beaker Period

Metal first arrived in Britain around 2400 BC and it was brought to these shores by people who used a very particular type of pottery vessel that was used to hold a special brew that people would drink. These vessels were evidently special

gure 44. (left)
cavation of the
iff face (Site 2, see
gure 6) to record
chaeological
mains eroding out
 the peat.

gure 45. (right) The
rly Neolithic stone
earth revealed in
e cliff edge where
 would have been
ashed away if
cavation did not
ke place.

objects as they were chosen to be placed in the tombs of their dead. These pots are called 'Beakers' and hence why this period of early metal use is often termed the 'Beaker period'. The early part of the Beaker period is sometimes also called the 'Chalcolithic', which means 'Copper-Stone-Age', as copper is the main early metal that was worked, but stone tools still remained in use alongside it.

At Low Hauxley the burial cairn in the cliff face proved to be a fascinating example of a Beaker period burial monument with the earliest evidence yet for a 'Beaker' burial in the region. The cairn measured 17 metres in diameter and was around 1.5 metres above the old ground surface at it highest point, although just over half of the cairn had already been lost over the cliff edge. The excavation of the cairn proved a time-consuming ordeal as the sand had to be carefully removed from above each and every stone comprising the cairn. This was achieved by a combination of trowelling and brushing and the painstaking cleaning of the gaps in between the stones, a job ably achieved by the enthusiastic students and volunteers. Once the cairn was exposed we could make out a clear kerb running around its outer edge, but closer inspection of the body of the cairn material hinted at another kerb set within the first one defining a smaller, more circular, cairn. This was exciting as it raised the possibility that we were dealing with a multi-phase monument. Interest had also been piqued as I had found a few tiny sherds from a decorated pottery vessel in the voids between some of the cairn stones in the area where the earliest inner cairn appeared to have been subsequently modified. With this clue pointing to disturbance of the inner cairn we then systematically took the cairn apart phase by phase.

As we took the cairn apart some previously disturbed cists were identified, including one that had been built as part of the first extension to the original inner cairn and this had some fragments of human bone and pottery sherds of a later type of pottery, known as a 'Food Vessel', associated with it. A third phase of the cairn could be identified which took the form of an extension that wrapped itself around the entire cairn and was edged by the outer kerb that we had first noticed. It was this area of the cairn extension that had covered the small cist with cremated human remains and the pit with the human cremation and broken Food Vessel that we had excavated with Jim Nesbitt from the cliff face in 2009.

Figure 46. The burial cairn under excavation in summn 2013 with the stone exposed after cleaning off the san (2m scale).

ure 47. The
ial cairn during
cavation showing
 stone kerbs
ating to the
ferent phases of
nstruction.

But the discoveries did not stop there.

As we started to take the inner cairn down Jim Brightman rolled over a large boulder close to the centre of the cairn which lay above, and slightly to the side, of the pit that had contained the cist which had contained the young man with the longer-necked of the two Beaker vessels found in 1993. As he rolled the boulder upwards to grasp it for removal he shouted over in jubilation that he had discovered some prehistoric rock art! I shouted back in approval as rock art is not only one of my passions but it also signified this as a special burial monument indeed.

The rock art consisted of three 'cup marks' connected by a linear groove, all of which had been pecked on to one of the flat sides of a hefty sandstone boulder. The boulder had broken across one of the cup marks either before, or when, it had been placed in the cairn leaving a fresh-looking break, and this contrasted with the much more weathered appearance of the rock art and the rest of the rock surface. This was significant as it indicated that the rock had been carved long before and had been left in an open landscape context, exposed to the elements, before it was selected for inclusion in the cairn when one end of it had broken off. Therefore the rock art itself was much older than the cairn in which it had been placed.

Another notable observation was that the stone had been placed so that the rock art faced downwards towards the burial, signifying not only the direct association of the rock art with the deceased but also

ure 48. One of
 disturbed burial
ts found within
 body of the
rn in which small
gments of human
ne and pottery
re found.

ure 49. (right) The
le cup-marked
ulder found in the
rn.

Figure 50. Plan of the cairn showing the different phases of construction.

Figure 51. The whetstone or 'hone' found next to the cup-marked rock above the primary burial.

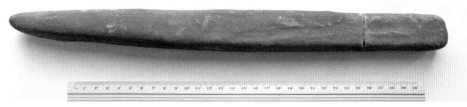

the intention of the cairn builders that the rock was never to be seen again.

With the sun beating down and spirits high with all these discoveries it was Jim Nesbitt's turn to ratchet up the discoveries. Jim approached me a day or so later to tell me that he had found a smoothed stone falling out of the cliff section within the cairn material above the 1993 cist void, next to where we had found the cup-marked rock, a few weeks before the excavation had started. I asked him if he could bring it back to site for me to have a look at in case it was something important. Jim of course obliged and he unwrapped from his packaging this long stone in front of me wondering if I thought it was of interest – it turned out to be the best prehistoric whetstone, or hone, that I had ever seen!

This was a long square-sectioned piece of fine-grained sandstone with a more round-sectioned handle, and which had been carefully shaped to allow for long sharpening strokes, presumably for metal blades, in much the same way as we sharpen a kitchen knife today using a sharpening steel. This provided proxy evidence for the use of metal by the Low Hauxley Beaker community and echoed the discovery of a small bronze dagger from a burial in a very similar cairn that had been recorded eroding from the cliff face three kilometres further up the coast at Amble by William Greenwell in 1883. The position of this 'offering' next to the cup-marked rock was surely no coincidence and together these objects, both with presumable religious and symbolic significance, emphasise the importance accorded to the first burial on the site. Small caches of limpet shells were found around the

Figure 52. The small bronze dagger and two of the Food Vessel pots with human remains found in the cairn excavated below the sand dunes at Amble in 1883.

cairn and amongst the rocks of the cairn extensions. Radiocarbon dating of one of the shell caches showed it had been deposited when the cairn was in use which suggests that these deposits of shellfish were perhaps offerings to the dead made by the participants in the funerary ritual.

When we undertook radiocarbon dating on the various sets of human remains and combined these dates with the positions from which they had come within the cairn it became clear that the monument had three distinct structural phases that dated from c.2400–1800 BC. Overall it looks as though this burial monument was in use for around 500–600 years making it a long-lived monument that would have featured as a landmark and important place for the local community over around 20 generations. From around 1800 BC it seems to have gone out of use and this is supported by the fact that turf began to grow over the lower edges of the cairn so that only the highest central area of stones protruded.

Bronze Age

The Bronze Age spans the period 1800–700 BC and is a time usually associated with highly organised farming communities and the laying out of field systems across the landscape.

The evidence for this period on the site at Low Hauxley is slight, but it shows the presence of people and the burning of grasses, presumably as part of agricultural activities. The evidence included a pit that had been dug for an unknown purpose that contained a charred twig and the dating of two charred grass stems from the associated soil. The cairn had gone out of use at this time and the ground may have been brought into use as pasture or, at times, possibly for cultivation. The area occupied by the burial cairn appears, therefore, to have lost its significance as a place for burial and become incorporated as farmland.

At the end of the Bronze Age the stone-founded building that Jim Nesbitt had photographed in the cliff face was constructed on top of the black peat which had evidently dried out by this time. The top of the peat had been dated to the centuries around the beginning of the first millennium BC and so the house had to be after that date. The wooden peg that had been driven into the top of the peat next to the stone building was dated to somewhere between 800 and 540 BC and this and the stone building are likely to date to the same time (ie. they are 'contemporary' with each other).

Shortly after this date, however, another catastrophic environmental change

Figure 53. The stone founded building situated above the peat with what appears to be a sunken floor and pit within its interior (© Nick Best).

Figure 54. One of the Iron Age stone-lined hearths discovered on the site.

affected the near-shore area as sand was blown inland in vast quantities so as to completely cover all of the Bronze Age ground surface along what is now the coastal strip of Druridge Bay, and it covered most of the Beaker period burial cairn and the smaller cairn that Clive Bonsall had excavated, and also covered the Late Bronze Age–Early Iron Age stone building Jim had photographed in the cliff face. Over a metre of sand was deposited and this in effect killed the existing soil and prevented any further growth of vegetation on it.

The function of the stone building remains unknown but the low walls and the presence of an internal pit, possibly a hearth or fire pit, compare well with the form that settlements of this period take and which are known from elsewhere in Northumberland, particularly the Cheviot uplands, where stone-founded circular buildings of Late Bronze Age and Early Iron Age date can still be seen as surface remains.

Iron Age-Roman

Once the windblown sand had been dumped along the coastal margin these dunes eventually stabilised and attracted a vegetation cover that continued to build in thickness throughout the Iron Age so that a sandy soil developed. Around 300 BC or slightly earlier a stone-lined hearth was constructed as part of a house set back from the cliff edge. The slabs of flat stone used to construct this hearth appear to have been robbed from the top of the burial cairn, as the flat stones of the later phase cists offered an easy quarry for useful building stone. The remains of this hearth were discovered on the site during the machining off of the overburden and could be easily recognised by the scorched-reddened colour of the stone slabs. Excavation through the layers of ash debris within the hearth allowed samples of charred wood to be obtained from which radiocarbon measurements

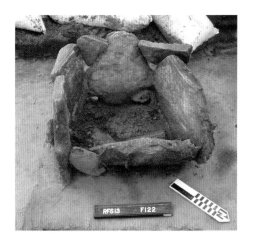

were made. The lower fill of ash was dated to the Late Iron Age, *c.*350–200 BC, whilst the upper fill of ash was dated to *c.*AD 170–325 placing the latter in the Roman period after Hadrian's Wall had been constructed, and which lies 38 kilometres to the south.

These remains were found in the westernmost corner of the main excavation site and the remains continued under the baulk edge of the trench which meant that not all of this settlement could be excavated. Their discovery was wholly unexpected as there had never been any prior indication that remains of the Iron Age would survive on the site, although John Davies had found a few sherds of Roman pottery in the cliff face during the 1980s. What could be recorded included a sequence of drip gullies and structural building slots defining several phases of timber building construction together with a well-preserved area of external paving on the seaward side of the building. This is what we would today call a patio and, just like us, the inhabitants of the site placed it outside the entrance so as to command a wonderful sea view. The flat sandstone slabs used to construct the paved area are thought to have come from the burial cairn, which was only a few yards away, and would have provided a ready source of flat stones and this could account for why the small cists in the upper parts of the cairn that we encountered during its excavation were disturbed and had slabs missing. Other stone-lined hearth pits were also found in and around the area of these buildings as well as over towards the cairn where the hearth pits had just been cut into the sand. Radiocarbon dates from the various constructional features suggest the site was continuously occupied from the mid to late Iron Age through to the second or third century AD. One of the house-construction gullies produced some sherds of Samian Ware Roman pottery, produced in Gaul (modern-day France), as well as native British pottery and large quantities of shellfish and animal bone testifying to a varied, and apparently, rich diet which included exotic imports from the Roman empire. A well-preserved and finely-made bone pin was discovered from the house deposits together with a copper alloy ring or washer indicating a fairly sophisticated economy for the residents of this settlement.

The site at Low Hauxley lies to the north of Hadrian's Wall on the border with, or within, the lands of the tribe known as the 'Votadini' by the Romans. They are thought to have been one of the tribes that entered into a compact with the Emperor Claudius when he landed his Roman army in southern England and agreed not to oppose him. As a consequence the Votadini are thought to have been a 'client' kingdom of Rome and this is thought to be one of the reasons why there is a remarkable absence of Roman forts in Votadinian territory, even when the Romans advanced north for short periods into what is today Scotland. The Iron Age-Roman evidence from Low Hauxley, although meagre as only a part of the site could be excavated, suggests that farming communities in the Votadinian territory north of Hadrian's Wall may have experienced some benefits from their position on the edge of the Roman empire as they could participate in the trade and exchange

Figure 55. The Iron Age stone paving in the foreground situated immediatel, outside the Iron Age house looking out to sea.

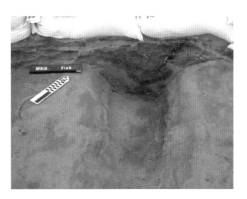

Figure 56. (left) The remains of a timber circular structure (black ring) with a central discolouration which is possibly a scorched area where a fireplace had once been pre-dating the stone paving.

Figure 57. (right) An excavated section of a gully associated with a Roman period Roundhouse overlying the Iron Age ones that produced Roman pottery and food waste in the form of animal bone and seafood shells.

of goods with merchants from within the empire whilst still enjoying, for the most part, their traditional way of life. In return, however, they may have been required to pay tribute to Rome and/or provide a military 'buffer' from the hostile kingdoms further to the north.

Trying to get a handle on the sequence of the sediments at the site still remained problematic so I took samples of organic material from as many levels as possible. To try and work out when the Roman period occupation and its contemporary soil layer went out of use I submitted a limpet shell fragment from the very top of the Roman period soil for radiocarbon dating and this returned a date of c.357–439 AD. This was helpful as it meant that at, or shortly after, this date the entire coastal strip suffered yet another catastrophic inundation of windblown sand, this time several metres thick. This appears to have coincided with the end of the Roman presence in Britain and the beginning of the period popularly known

as the 'Dark Ages', or in academic circles as the 'early medieval' period. This thick layer of sand again killed the soil below and created a system of extensive sandy dunes. Eventually the dunes stabilised and a turf mat took root and eventually a thin soil developed.

Medieval

The soil above the sand dunes blown in during the Dark Ages had formed by the medieval period and this would have given rise to a coastal dune landscape very similar to that of today, although the cliff face is likely to have been a few dozen metres further out around most of Druridge Bay. After the 2013 archaeological excavation a longstanding chum of mine, Alison Sheridan, at the National Museum of Scotland had agreed to look at the Beaker pottery, being a renowned expert in the subject, and in my discussions with her Alison recollected that she thought the museum had some bone

Figure 58. Roman pottery recovered from the gully.

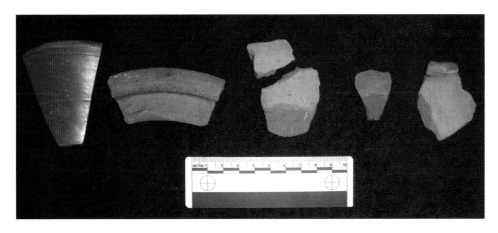

Figure 59. General view of the excavations underway during summer 2013.

from the Low Hauxley area. It turned out that a doctor from Edinburgh had been holidaying in the area in the 1950s and had found some human bone eroding from the cliffs and had collected it and taken it back to Edinburgh with him and subsequently deposited it with the museum. Alison and I agreed to get a sample of the bone radiocarbon dated and the date came back as c.AD 1435–1459, a very tight dating span in the middle of the 15th century, so a generation after the battle of Agincourt and immediately prior to the War of the Roses in the period of the climatic downturn known as the 'Little Ice Age'.

This was interesting as there was no way this body could have come from the deeply buried early prehistoric soil layer or the Iron Age-Roman soil layer. Neither could it be from the modern soil layer as this is too young. This could only leave the soil layer above the Dark Age sand deposit which means that the Dark Age dune system appears to have stabilised and a soil developed sometime prior to the 15th century creating the conditions for an interment to be made.

We still had a mystery to solve however: what on earth were those rock cut pits on the foreshore for? I had promised

Figure 60. School students embarking on the excavation o one of the rock cut pits on the foreshore

Jim Nesbitt I would look into this one when I had met him on the beach after he had sent me the first email back in 2009. During the 2013 excavations I despatched a party of school students to start digging a section through the fill of one of the pits whilst the tide was out. They worked hard, as it was heavy work, and as the excavation proceeded and I went over to check on progress it became clear that these pits were not shallow affairs, but in fact went down some way in excess of one and a half metres. Time was not on their side and despite a valiant effort the tide came back in and the excavation had to be abandoned until the following day. The next day came and we had no students available so as soon as the tide was out Philippa and Kate set-to on re-excavating the material that had been washed back into the pit. The afternoon came and the tide turned so we were once again in a race against time. I went to check progress and as it was tiring work it fell to me to push the excavation on. Whilst excavating Jim Brightman had noticed an interesting feature though: at one end of the pit on the rock wall he had noticed an 'X' carved into the rock. With this in mind I ploughed on excavating into an ever-expanding void that kept filling with water. This made excavation awkward but with the assistance of a team of willing bucket carriers I was able to complete the section to a depth where we could see what was going on. Once the upper fill of beach cobble and shingle was removed the fill became greyer and blacker and once into this material it became clear this was coal slag and mining waste. The pits had been cut through the layer of sandstone bedrock, which was only a foot or so thick and very soft due to having been kept damp as a result of being in the intertidal zone, and below that it came on to a seam of coal that had been quarried out. The coal void was wider than the rectangular hole that had been punctured through the overlying sandstone. These were bellpits for coal mining and the rectangular cuts through the sandstone were the base of the shafts that had been sunk through the sand dunes which would have overlain these rock 'steels' in the past prior to the coast being eroded back to its present position. The pits opened out below the sandstone where the coal was scraped out and they had backfilled the pits with the waste material. Bell pit mining is typically a medieval method of coal extraction and this made sense of the 'X' carved on to the face of the sandstone wall as this can be likened to the 'mason's marks' that were commonly made on quarried stone blocks dressed for use in medieval structures, such as those that can still be seen on Newcastle's medieval town walls or in the walls of local castles, pele towers and churches.

But there was a final twist. Within the main excavation trench on the cliff edge we had observed a broadly circular feature towards the back edge of the trench with a pale sandy fill. We strung out two perpendicular string sections across the feature and started to excavate two of the opposed quadrants so we could understand the profile and fill of the feature. As we excavated this feature it became clear that the side of the pit was not very weathered and the fill had no finds of any sort in it, no organic material and the fill had been dumped into the feature in a series of deposits, probably from baskets, buckets or barrows as slight differentiations in the colour and composition of the fill could be noted. But the feature went on and on and the sides remained vertical. It became clear, then, that this was a shaft of some sort and a relatively recent one at that, archaeologically speaking. Being just 40 metres inland from the rock cut pits on the foreshore the obvious conclusion was that this was the shaft to another bell pit, but one that still had the upper part of its shaft intact because the cliff edge had not yet receded that far back. So taken together we were able to solve the mystery for Jim Nesbitt and confidently interpret this unusual cluster of rock cut pits as the remains of medieval coal mining.

Sometime in the late medieval or post-medieval period yet another large-scale inundation of windblown sand was dumped on the coastal strip and the medieval soil was buried and the vegetation cover killed off. In time this sand dune

Figure 63. Excavatio underway of the mineshaft within the cliff face excavation site (vertical scale = 2m).

stabilised and was colonised by plants and a marram grass turf layer developed. This thin soil with grass cover continues to this day and forms the modern ground surface that we are familiar with.

At the end of the excavation we cleared the site and brought Stuart and the team from Straughan's back in for the painstaking job of backfilling the trench and regrading it so that it blended back into the cliff line. Within less than a year the soil had completely vegetated over again and the compacted fill of the trench had stabilised. This had proved a useful excavation in more ways than one as we had been able to test a technique for excavating a deep cliff edge environment, and the careful use of large plant to strip a substantial and deep area, that realistically could not have otherwise been done by hand, had paid off archaeologically. But it had also demonstrated how it could be restored quickly too, and the grassland environment able to recover.

Figure 64. Recordin the different layers c sediments in the clif face before the tide came in.

5. Making Sense of Things

Although the excavations at Low Hauxley had uncovered far more than was originally anticipated, including remains from periods for which there was no prior suggestion, we had little choice but to leave the site without having excavated all of the remains that survive below this stretch of sand dunes.

Because our original trench layout had been based around the known archaeology, that is the burial cairn with underlying Mesolithic remains situated on a raised hillock, the discovery of more widespread remains on the site that were not known about meant that the trench had not extended far enough to include all of these other remains. The surviving Mesolithic site is probably about half-excavated as it could clearly be seen to continue below the south and west baulks of the excavation trench, although it remains unknown of course how much of this site once existed to seaward. It occupies the top of the raised hillock and the distribution of chipped flints could be traced in the buried soil exposed in the cliff face for 17 metres southwards from the trench edge before flints become absent.

Most of the Iron Age-Roman site is still to be excavated as we only encountered one segment of it in the south-west corner of the main excavation trench; the rest of it continuing under the baulk here. This settlement is set back from the present cliffs by around 20 metres and therefore it is unlikely that any of this has yet been lost to the sea and so any subsequent excavation should be able to relocate and record the rest of this site prior to its destruction by the retreating cliff face.

Although there are many questions arising from this excavation the ones that I will attempt to address concern the Mesolithic settlement and understanding the Beaker period burial cairn and its significance.

Mesolithic Settlement

Why do the earliest settlements at Low Hauxley and Howick date to around 8000 BC, why are they both coastal and why do they have evidence for circular huts around six metres in diameter and both have the same kind of stone tool kits? Why do they both have bevelled pebble tools associated with them and also fragments of ochreous material?

These questions, though puzzling, deserve serious attention as other directly comparable Mesolithic coastal settlements of this type have recently been found at East Barns near Dunbar and at Echline on the south side of the Firth of Forth. To answer these questions we have to start by considering what the geography of this region looked like at this time. This subject is known as 'palaeogeography' and, as will become clear, without a full appreciation of it an accurate history of Britain during the Mesolithic would not only be impossible, but also misleading.

Earlier in this book we considered the history of landscape evolution since the last Ice Age and the drowning of huge swathes of landscape as the North Sea was formed and the once-inhabited land was inundated and eventually buried by the sea. In recent years there has been a surge in research dedicated to understanding sea level change and the complexities associated with modelling how and why the land comprising the North Sea Basin became submerged and Britain changed from being a far-flung peninsula of North West Europe to a littoral of islands off the European coast.

During the period 8400–7800 BC climate change proxies show a period of rapid temperature rise and a corresponding rapid rise in sea level. This can be seen in the large-scale spread of hazel throughout northern Britain at this time and in the climate records from ice cores, such as those from Greenland. Although sea level had been on a continuous rising trajectory for the previous 6500 years there were periods when it rose more rapidly than others, primarily due to increases in annual average temperatures, and it is in this period in the latter 9th millennium and early 8th millennium BC that just such a pulse of sea level rise occurred. The speed of this rise meant that people would have been aware of it within their own lifetimes and large tracts of low lying ground will have been lost. As large swathes of the North Sea Basin became inundated in the shallows of the encroaching North Sea, people living on the coastal margins of these lands may have been prompted to move further afield to higher ground safe from the threat of the rising sea and, no doubt, occasional storm surges. Could our Mesolithic coastal settlements of North East Britain relate to such a

population displacement?

The early North East coast Mesolithic sites at Low Hauxley, Howick, East Barns, Echline, Filpoke Beacon and Crammond all date to between 8400 and 7800 BC and so correlate with this period of large-scale landscape inundation of the northern North Sea. Correlation, however, does not necessarily equate to causation, so to test this idea we need to see what other lines of evidence reveal to see if there is convergence of independent data. These sites form a distinctive group that share much in common and in this regard it is striking that they all share precisely the same flint technology based on the manufacture of 'narrow blade' microliths and utilisation of the local beach pebble flint. The style in which microliths are manufactured has long been argued to be a mechanism by which cultural affinities are displayed. In other words, people sharing the same microlith styles are typically thought to be connected as part of a larger social group. Equally striking, however, is the similarity in form of several of these settlements.

Until the discovery at Howick Mesolithic 'houses' were virtually unknown in Britain. In the few years that have passed since that discovery directly similar houses have been found elsewhere on the North East British coast at East Barns and Echline, and also on the Isle of Man at Cass ny Hawin; and a similar site, although originally interpreted in a slightly different way, had been known from the estuary at Mount Sandel in Northern Ireland since the late 1970s. The plan form of the houses is remarkable as they are all in the region of six metres in diameter, they all have scooped or 'sunken' internal floor areas, they all show evidence of several phases of build/rebuild, they all have central hearth areas, they all were occupied by people using a narrow blade microlith technology, they are all

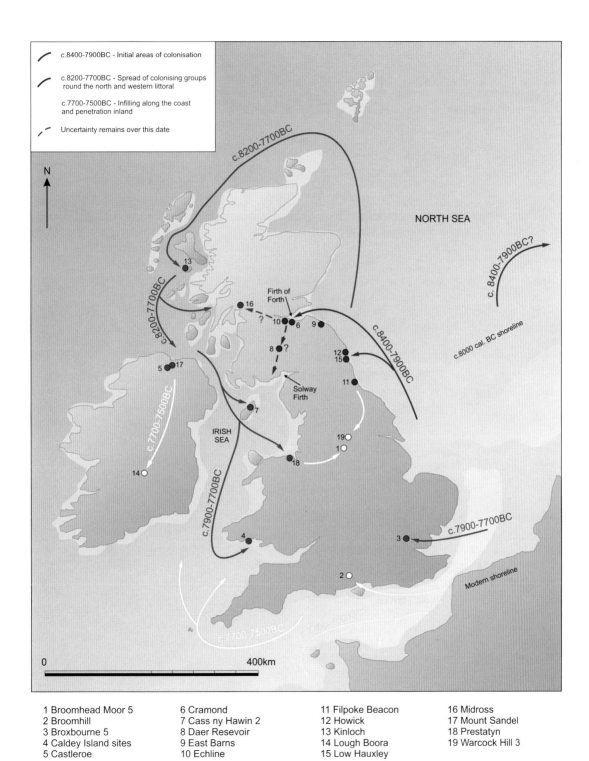

Figure 65. Model showing the displacement of Mesolithic 'narrow blade' microlith-using groups from the North Sea Plain into Britain.

1 Broomhead Moor 5
2 Broomhill
3 Broxbourne 5
4 Caldey Island sites
5 Castleroe
6 Cramond
7 Cass ny Hawin 2
8 Daer Resevoir
9 East Barns
10 Echline
11 Filpoke Beacon
12 Howick
13 Kinloch
14 Lough Boora
15 Low Hauxley
16 Midross
17 Mount Sandel
18 Prestatyn
19 Warcock Hill 3

coastal or estuarine, and they all date to the period 8400–7700 BC. They have typically produced bevelled pebble tools and ochreous material and several have produced seal bone. Given the convergence of these different threads of evidence we can therefore make a link between the people occupying and settling these coastal locations around the northern British Isles at this time.

Understanding who these people were and where they came from demands a closer look. The presence of bevelled pebble tools is significant as these are almost entirely a coastal phenomenon in Mesolithic Britain and this would suggest they are a tool associated with coastal tasks and coastal living. When studying the bevelled pebble tools I had excavated at Howick I had investigated their distribution, the wear patterns, ethnographic parallels and experimental work and had also had some residue analysis performed on the working edge of one of the tools.

Observing the distribution of bevelled pebbles in Wales and South West England, the late and distinguished archaeologist Roger Jacobi made the point that the coastal distribution of these tools can be correlated closely with the breeding colonies of grey seal and he drew attention to the high meat and fat content of these mammals, as well as the suitability of their pelts for making skin boats. A similar correlation can also be made for the British North East coast where there is also a direct correlation with the sites that have produced bevelled pebble tools (Low Hauxley, Howick, Ness End and East Barns) and the breeding grounds of grey seal.

Seal skins are tough and waterproof making them ideal for skin boat construction, but they also insulate well which means they make particularly warm clothing. Seal skin boats have been widely used around the arctic rim,

from Siberia to Greenland, since records began. In fact the Yupik and Inuit of North America still use seal skins to make their lightweight and highly effective umiaks and kayaks, the former being the large open boats used for whale and walrus hunting and the latter being the covered-in two-man boat.

The rock 'steels' that lie immediately beyond the Low Hauxley site are well known grey seal basking and breeding grounds and it is no coincidence that on the day the 2013 excavation started a dead grey seal was washed up on the rocky shore immediately in front of the excavation site. A further dead seal was found on the beach further down the bay a few months later. The pattern of wear on the Howick and Low Hauxley tools showed they had been held at an angle and employed in a forwards and backwards rubbing motion. The residue analysis on the Howick specimen showed that it had traces of meat or fat on it, consistent with its use on animal skins. The exploitation of seal at our Mesolithic North East coastal sites could therefore have involved far more than just taking them for their meat and fat.

The discovery of ochreous material at Low Hauxley and Howick in the same contexts as the bevelled pebble tools is noteworthy. The American coastal Chumash tribe are recorded as having used ochre as part of a mastic that was spread on the sewn joints of seal skin-covered boats to caulk them. When heated and mixed with pine resin ochre acts as a fixative so the resulting mastic can be used as a caulking agent or glue. The presence of ochre and flint punching tools associated with hearths on early Holocene (ie. Mesolithic) coastal settlements in California has led American archaeologists to interpret this as evidence for boatbuilding amongst these early Holocene groups. At both Low Hauxley and Howick the ochreous material was also associated with the hearth areas, as well as the bevelled pebble tools. It is also worth mentioning that three of the four flint piercing/punching tools (borers and awls) found at Low Hauxley were from the Mesolithic hut deposits or just next to it, whilst ten awls were found in the house occupation deposits at Howick around the central hearth pits.

Taking the Low Hauxley and Howick evidence for bevelled pebble tools, ochre, flint awls, coastal setting and the proximity of seal basking rock platforms together it is suggestive of the construction and/or maintenance of seagoing skin boats at both Low Hauxley and Howick. I concluded, therefore, that the taking of grey seal and the use of their skins to make seagoing boats was likely to have been a key feature of these pioneer northern British coastal Mesolithic communities.

Another observation struck me as I read through the excavation reports of the various sites: why did none of them, with the exception of Echline, have any deer bone associated with them? Deer bone, specifically red deer and roe deer, is normally quite common on British Mesolithic sites and certainly the inland sites. Could it be that terrestrial fauna was simply hard to catch when living in a coastal location?

In the hearths at Howick though I had found not just seal bone but also the bone of wild pig, fox and dog/wolf, so it is clear these people could have taken deer if they had wanted to. Could it be that what we were witnessing here was a cultural preference of these narrow blade-using coastal groups to base their economy on seal and other near-coastal resources whilst deliberately avoiding preying on the deer?

Excavation of inland British Mesolithic sites has shown that groups using a different type of microlith style, collectively known as 'broad blade microliths', had settled in Britain and occupied its interior since the end of the last Ice Age and a feature of these sites is that in most cases they appear to be geared around a terrestrial meat-based economy with deer being crucial to their way of life. This is no better exemplified than at the lake-edge settlement at Star Carr in North Yorkshire where an assemblage of deer frontlets (ie. the front part of the skull), still with their antler attached, was found with eye-holes carved into them indicating their use as face masks. Evidently deer symbolism and ritual was fundamental to these earlier inland Mesolithic groups.

Could the avoidance of deer by the coastal narrow blade groups at Low Hauxley and the other sites have been a taboo or, more interestingly, could this have arisen because the already resident inland hunter-gatherer groups relied on this resource and so the narrow blade-using seal hunters deliberately resisted from preying upon deer in order to avoid conflict? The more I thought about this the more this possibility found appeal as it could explain a pattern that has emerged in the archaeological record whilst also reconciling how geographically widespread groups with different diets and economic practices could co-exist in landscapes that were rapidly changing and when competition for land and resources may have been increased due to the loss of land to the North Sea.

Considering the circumstantial evidence for the use of skin boats by the narrow blade-using coastal groups, the siting of their settlements adjacent to seal basking grounds, the uniformity of the sites, their shared use of cultural symbols (microliths) and economic practices and the focus on coastal and near-shore resources (e.g. beach flint), together with their appearance on North East British shores at the same time that the adjacent land in the North Sea Plain was being inundated, allows for a good case to be made that our Mesolithic residents at Low Hauxley, Howick and the other coastal sites were in fact colonisers, or refugees to put it a different way, who had abandoned the inundated lands of the North Sea Plain and moved further back to higher ground from drowned areas further out in what is now the North Sea.

In other words, could our earliest residents at Low Hauxley be people who had lived further out in the North Sea Plain before being displaced and finding a new home on what is today the Northumberland coast? At this time, c.8000 BC, Britain was still connected to Europe via a swathe of land that extended from East Yorkshire and East Anglia all the way across to what is now Belgium, Holland and the German Bight. There would have been some islands too and there was a deep inlet off the coast from Holderness which palaeogeographers call the 'Outer Silver Pit' (see Figure 17).

The Mesolithic people who lived at Low Hauxley occupied a dry hillock that would have looked out over a coastal plain with the shoreline perhaps up to a kilometre further out than it is today. They were probably from the same cultural grouping as their neighbours further up the coast at Howick and they would have identified with each other and followed a very similar way of life. Over time the groups who had settled on Britain's North East coast spread further reaching the North West coast, Northern Ireland, the Isle of Man and North Wales within just a few centuries. The deer hunters of the interior continued using their broad blade technology during this time and the population density across Britain will have risen throughout the 8th millennium BC. At Low Hauxley the radiocarbon dates associated with the various pits show that Mesolithic occupation continued here, although perhaps not continuously, for a period

extending over at least 700 years and perhaps longer.

The lack of remains from the later Mesolithic is curious and invites us to question whether this could also be in some way associated with the huge environmental changes that took place during the Mesolithic. When we consider the other coastal Mesolithic sites of North East and North West Britain there is an absence of dated remains from this time, particularly the centuries around 6200 BC. We know that 6200 BC is a crucial staging point in the history of the North Sea and the British Isles as this is when the catastrophic tsunami known as the Storegga Slide raced across the sea from the Norwegian coast, erupting onto north British shores and those of the large island known as 'Doggerland' and its smaller relatives. This catastrophic inundation is likely to have been the event that breached the remaining 'land bridge' which thereby made Britain an island (see above, Chapter 2).

The conspicuous lack of dated Mesolithic sites on northern British shorelines from 6200 BC and the next few centuries could possibly be a result of sample bias and the fact that such sites have just not been found yet, or as is considered more likely here, this lack of evidence could reflect a population collapse following the impact of a tsunami that changed their world.

It is notable that from around this time onwards the styles of microliths that became adopted in North West Europe are markedly different to the types of microliths that are found in Britain. This is referred to as the 'Trapeze Horizon' in Europe and it is a phenomenon that is entirely absent from Britain implying some degree of cultural separation, and perhaps isolation, for the Mesolithic groups who survived in what had become 'Island Britain'.

Understanding the impact of Storegga

on the human populations around the North Sea Basin, including those on Doggerland, the other North Sea islands, the isthmus connecting Britain to the Continent as well as the surrounding coastlines, is in its infancy. It is, however, a serious question that must be addressed by future research if we are to ever gain an understanding of our origins as an island nation. At Low Hauxley, the landscape did eventually recover and a woodland comprising alder with occasional elm, oak, hazel and birch developed around the site by c.5400 BC. The sea level continued to rise, however, and by c.5000 BC the woodland floor became soft and wet and adults and children walked through it, perhaps following wild boar, wild cattle and red deer – as the footprints and hoofprints visible on the surface of what is now the foreshore peat at Low Hauxley indicate.

So despite the impact of Storegga people eventually returned and the landscape became settled again. It was only by around 4000 BC, however, that the sea level stabilised and Britain attained broadly the same shoreline with which we are familiar today.

Burial Cairn

The most visual part of the site at Low Hauxley was undoubtedly the burial cairn and given that this ancient monument had been giving up its secrets since 1983 it was no surprise that its excavation had raised much public interest. Ancient burial mounds date from the Neolithic, Beaker period and Bronze Age and, as a whole, are not particularly rare with several tens of thousands known throughout Britain.

The cairn at Low Hauxley, is, however, one of a select group of monuments as it is from a cairn group that dates specifically, and only, to the Beaker period. The primary burial at Low Hauxley is one of the earliest Beaker

dates so far available in northern Britain. Also, it has a clear structural sequence revealing associated changes in funerary ritual and mortuary practice as well as in the types of ceramics deposited with the burials. Moreover, having been covered over by metres of sand after it had gone out of use the surviving cairn was in good condition, relatively undisturbed (apart from the erosion by the sea and some stone robbing in the Iron Age) and with a geochemical environment that allowed for the survival of otherwise perishable material like unburnt human bone.

The burial monument appears to have been built by some of the first 'Beaker Folk' to arrive in Britain. The closest Continental parallels for the Low Hauxley Beakers are from the Rhineland, suggesting the source area for the people represented by these pots. Beakers were intimately associated with the first metalworking traditions in western Europe and their arrival on the shore of Northumberland heralds the arrival of metalworking knowledge to North East England. The deliberate placement of a long honing stone, akin to a modern sharpening steel, above one of the Beaker burials served to reference the deceased's connection with metalworking. Whetstones, which give blades their sharp edges, have long been attributed with magical properties and mythical power as witnessed by the whetstone that is thought to have been used as a 'sceptre' (symbol of kingship) that was found in the Anglo-Saxon boat burial at Sutton Hoo, or the legend of the 'Whetstone of Tudwal Tudglyd' from the Welsh manuscripts.

Similar Beaker burial sites have been discovered elsewhere along the Northumberland coast at Amble, Longhoughton, Howick and Beadnell but, apart from the site at Amble, none were as well preserved as the Low Hauxley cairn. These sites display a common pattern in that they are always in locally raised or prominent locations close to a freshwater estuary and overlooking the coast.

These are likely to be the monuments of the first metalworkers to come to this region and by siting them so that the monuments, and indeed the position of the deceased person in some cases, looked out to sea, from whence they had probably originated, a reference was perhaps being made to their homelands. These burial cairns would have also been conspicuous when approached from the sea and in the case of the Low Hauxley site we know from the palaeoenvironmental analysis that the burial mound had been

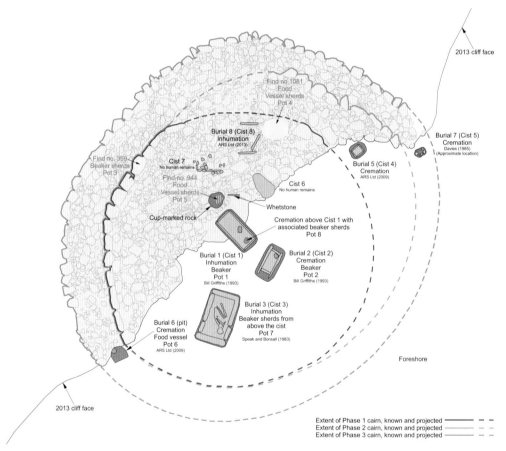

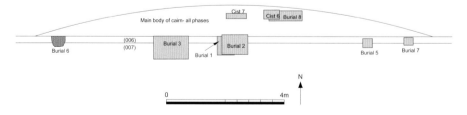

Figure 66. Plan of the burial cairn showing its phasing and estimated extent.

carefully positioned to occupy a raised knoll or hillock that stood above an area of wetland.

This meant that the burial ground was set apart from the landscape in which people lived and farmed, being separated by water. It occupied a transitional area between dry land and the sea, a sort of 'in-between' land. This could have been considered both metaphor and practical reality for separating the spirits of the dead from the living. The spirits of the dead may have been thought to occupy a twilight world that was in neither the living world nor the underworld, but a liminal world between the two. The idea that spirits could be kept at bay by water has a long pedigree and the positioning of the burial cairn on what was in effect a small island protruding from a wetland was perhaps a way of keeping the spirits in a confined place where they could not disturb the people in nearby settlements as they went about their everyday lives.

The inclusion of the cup-marked rock in the cairn next to the whetstone is also an important symbol. This was an already ancient object with religious and symbolic power but one that belonged to an earlier people who had long inhabited Britain. So why did these Beaker people see fit to take one of these carved stones and incorporate it into their burial monument with the rock art face down towards the deceased?

The impulse at work here seems to be one geared towards drawing on the power of these ancient symbols whilst also claiming the sanction of the ancient indigenous traditions. The act of placing the rock art above the deceased may have been an attempt to confer the ancient magic of the landscape on to the Beaker migrant to protect him from any harmful local spirits.

Whatever the true purpose for including the carved rock we shall probably never know but at a general level we can perceive an incoming group of cult specialists with the knowledge of how to transform stone into metal trying to align themselves with, and draw power from, what was by then an ancient form of symbolism in their adopted home. Appropriating these ancient markings in a public way by including them in the tombs of their dead may have been a way of legitimising the arrival of these early metalworkers who brought with them their new ways and sacred knowledge, but ones which referenced the ancient traditions of the land they had come to.

The cairn at Low Hauxley had further burials deposited within it over the course of several centuries and this included extending the cairn on two occasions in order to fit in more burials. As time went on the mortuary practice changed from inhumation of fleshed people to cremation and, by the time the cairn was extended, this was accompanied by a distinct change to a new kind of pottery.

By around 2000 BC Beakers were no longer being deposited in the cairn and a new type of ceramic known as 'Food Vessels' was being placed with the interments. These have a very different shape to Beakers being more like a vase with a narrow base and an upright upper body. They are heavily decorated and can share some decorative styles and motifs with Beakers but are otherwise quite distinct, having a typically thicker fabric. Similar to Beakers, though, they are thought to have contained food or liquid to accompany the spirit of the dead person into the afterlife. The decoration and form of Food Vessels recalls a more ancient form of British pottery that had been used many hundreds of years before and it has been suggested by some archaeologists that the creators of the Food Vessels could have been deliberately harking back to this earlier tradition as part of an attempt to re-impose a set of traditional beliefs and practices as a response to the imposition of the new traditions that arrived when the first Beaker Folk brought their own cult practices with them.

This idea could have some merit as the arrival of metal technology was undoubtedly disruptive, but it probably only involved the arrival of relatively small numbers of people who may have been invited or welcomed over, as there is little suggestion in the archaeological record for a violent invasion at this time. Once the metalworking knowledge spread beyond the incoming group it would not be inconceivable that the indigenous communities sought to reassert their power and an effective way of doing this was to put a stop to the Beaker cult and replace it with a new one that referenced their own ancient traditions.

The latest use of Food Vessels at Low Hauxley, however, represents another change in the burial rite. The most recent of the dated burials, the one which Philippa had excavated from the cliff face in 2009, was a cremation that had been placed inside the Food Vessel.

Here we can see how the Food Vessel was no longer being used as an accompaniment to a burial but rather as a receptacle for holding the remains of the dead. This is a practice that has been noted at other burial cairns of similar age. This occurred around 1800 BC and represents the final use of this burial monument. After this date the dead were disposed of elsewhere suggesting that this monument and the people who were buried there were no longer considered relevant or important, as the cairn was allowed to grow over with turf so that only the uppermost stones poked through at the top. Quite why this happened can only be speculated upon but we know that from around this time onwards there was a massive expansion of farming into the uplands which must have coincided with a considerable expansion in population. The farmsteads that people built were situated amongst their paddocks and fields and they tended to bury their dead close by in small graves or cairns, no longer separated by water or other geographical features, but close to their homes on a local, family scale and not as large community-size monuments.

6. *A Community Strides Forth*

The Rescued from the Sea project benefited from a huge contribution by the local community. Situated in south-east Northumberland within the old coal mining belt the site at Low Hauxley is positioned between the coastal port of Amble to the north, Togston and Hadston to the west and Ellington and Ashington to the south.

Given the urgency of the project there was a relatively short lead-in time to galvanise community interest and support. This, however, did not pose a problem as once word started to get round interest levels soared and the project received considerable help and backing. This was also helped by the active promotion of the project by many local people who contributed their own knowledge, skills and networks to promote the work and encourage others to get involved.

So many people have been involved in this project that it is not possible to mention them all by name. We calculated that, including the school children, over 700 people took part in the physical excavation of the site, and still more people have been involved in some of the non-excavation activities. For any project this is a considerable number of people and with such a prodigious local involvement this excavation should stay in the consciousness of local people for several generations to come. The project has had widespread national coverage on television, in magazines and on the internet as well as local coverage on radio and in newspapers.

With the project having had such a high profile I am hopeful it has contributed to promoting and popularising the area and assisted, in some small way, in bringing the community together. Some people really went out of their way to assist the project and I have taken the liberty of mentioning a few of these local heroes below.

Figure 67. School children excavating animal prints and making plaster casts for identification in the classroom.

Figure 68. The Airplay youth group celebrating their excavation work with members of Channel 4's 'Time Team'.

One of the first people to draw my attention to the rich archaeology of Druridge Bay was Rodney Burge, a retired local lifeboat man, who discovered a pristine Bronze Age rapier in a rock pool on the foreshore at Low Hauxley after a heavy storm in the 1990s and which is now in the Great North Museum. I was delighted to see Rodney with his grandchildren when he visited the excavation site and he kindly fixed up for me to have a trip in a fishing boat so that I could photograph the excavation site from the sea.

Pauline 'the Posty' Jackson and Anne-

Marie Oliver were amazing throughout the project – always willing to do any job required whether filling sandbags, trowelling or helping with surveying. Barry, 'the Mattock', Mead arrived on site with his very own mattock clearly showing his intent and all credit is due to him for his assiduous dedication with the aforementioned tool and his good-humoured hard work during cleaning back the cliff face for recording. Irene Foggett, Callum Stone and Dave Cockcroft deserve a special mention being three of the many people who worked hard surveying thousands of flints as they were discovered during the

Figure 69. (left) John Craven from BBC's 'Countryfile' programme excavating with the team on the burial cairn.

Figure 70. Phil Harding from Channel 4's 'Time Team' filming a discussion with the author about the sediment sequence on the site.

Figure 71. Volunteers trowelling within the Mesolithic hut area, marking flints with white tags and surveying them.

trowelling back of the ancient buried soil. Master trowellers and beach monitors Davina Thompson, Alison Christer and 'Amble George' Martin were site regulars who contributed tirelessly throughout in all weather conditions. Brian Cosgrove at Hirst Park Middle School in Ashington did a sterling job bringing his media students to the site and shooting footage for a series of videoclips that they made and that have since been posted on the internet and have attracted large numbers of viewings (see http://hirstparkmiddle. org/index.php/rescued-from-the-sea).

Jim Bewley and Irene Foggett steadfastly took on the repetitive task of flotating all the soil samples with Laura Strafford and succeeded in recovering large quantities of charred hazelnut and other plant remains up to 10000 years old. Jim Nesbitt has been a real star, monitoring the site for the last ten years or so, and being so professional and pro-active in photographing the site, noticing features and artefacts as they eroded from the cliff face and in sending me information and keeping me updated on the site's changing condition. This project would

Figure 72. Volunteers excavating on the burial cairn.

probably not have happened if it wasn't for Jim's regular monitoring and his decision to send me the fateful email that alerted me to the parlous condition of the site and the other eroding remains.

John Davies kindly passed on to me his recollections of the site including the 1983 excavation and his monitoring work, his discovery of a fragmentary cist and cremation in 1985 as well as dedicated trowelling day after day on the 2013 excavation. There were many other marvellous efforts by the volunteers and it is unfortunate that there is not space to mention everyone here by name but their excellent work has been highly valued.

Since the excavation we have established a volunteer monitoring group who regularly walk the Druridge Bay coastline observing the cliff face for any sign of eroding archaeological remains and also for noting any wildlife or ecology that is under threat. They are a committed group and have already been successful in alerting us to a newly discovered area of eroding intertidal peat north of Cresswell covered in ancient hoofprints that dates to the Mesolithic period and the discovery of a small bronze ingot

Figure 73. The student film crew from Hirst Park Middle School.

that appears to have been washed out from the cliff face deposits before being deposited on the intertidal peat at Low Hauxley.

What struck me as being remarkable about the project while we were excavating on site was the incredible range of people that would turn up each

Figure 74. The volunteer coastal monitoring team (from left: Alison, Philippa, Steve, Bar George and Pauline

day to help. There were children from as young as four years old through to teenagers, students, young professionals, families, middle aged and the elderly, with some of the latter even in their 80s. What an incredible situation to see people of all these different ages working together in common endeavour and all enjoying the work, the camaraderie, helping each other and getting along together. People came from many different backgrounds too, ranging from all types of employment and education stages to youth groups, Guides and army cadets, and a wide range of retired people. Harnessing the skills that different people could bring to the table became a very valuable part of the project. In combination, Rescued from the Sea brought together local children and families, working professionals, the recently retired and elderly, Newcastle, Durham, Edinburgh, Stirling, Birmingham, Southampton and Glasgow Universities, the Northumberland

Wildlife Trust, the Great North Museum, local contractors, local schools, Druridge Bay Country Park, English Heritage, Natural England, Northumberland County Council, the British Museum, National Museum of Scotland, Channel 4's 'Time Team', the BBC and of course ourselves at Archaeological Research Services Ltd. Together we rescued an important part of not just the North East's, but the nation's, past in a way that would not have been possible without this extensive co-operation. The project's success is a testament to all of those who took part and contributed and I hope that everyone who has been involved realises that they have been an essential part of a big undertaking and have helped, whether in a big or small way, in rescuing part of our heritage.

7. LOOSE ENDS

The world does, of course, keep turning and since the main excavation in 2013 winter storms have hit the Druridge Bay coastline and cut the cliffs back further, in some places by over a metre.

The beach monitors have been busy, with Barry Mead finding a newly exposed peat shelf to the north of Cresswell at the south end of the Bay that was covered in hundreds of ancient animal hoofprints. We have taken samples from this peat and it dates to roughly 5000 BC in the late Mesolithic period. It is probably part of the same woodland as that represented by the intertidal peat at Low Hauxley at the north end of the Bay where we had the human and animal footprints. The storms also exposed the eroding Neolithic hearth in the cliff face to the north of the main excavation site. We mounted a small rescue excavation of this feature in March 2014 and this revealed the hearth with its associated charred wood, flint tools and chips dating to around 3600 BC.

There are evidently lots more archaeological and palaeoenvironmental remains surviving underneath the dunes that fringe Druridge Bay. These remains have been protected for thousands of years by the huge quantity of sand that has been blown over them and which has remained there for several thousand years. Now the sand is being washed away by the sea and the archaeological remains are being destroyed as sea level rises. There is no prospect of this process being halted and so we have to be vigilant and ready to react when more of these remains are exposed and subject to erosion.

When I reflect on this undertaking I am very aware that we have come a long way since I received that email from Jim Nesbitt in 2009. Back then we knew there was a Beaker period burial cairn, some evidence in the form of flint tools for Mesolithic activity and the photographs of enigmatic remains eroding from the cliff face and the unusual rock cut pits on the foreshore.

Since then we have unravelled the questions of what the various features were and through the scientific analysis of the various deposits, artefacts and structures we have been able to piece together a much longer and more detailed picture of what took place in this area over the last 10,000 years and how these findings fit into, and contribute to, our understanding of this period.

This particular coastal location is quite remarkable in that it has provided a touchstone for many of the key events in our national story – Mesolithic colonisers, arrival of the Neolithic, arrival of Beaker folk and the skills to work metal, Iron Age farmers who lived on the edge of the Roman empire, through to medieval coal mining. The preservation of these remains in a single deep stratigraphic sequence is almost unparalleled in British archaeology and it will therefore contribute to the future teaching of archaeological stratigraphy as it makes such a convenient case study.

Since excavating the site and working with other specialists to bring the site to publication there has been considerable interest shown. I have been asked to give numerous public lectures and papers to academic conferences throughout Britain and abroad on the project.

The Rescued from the Sea team has collaborated with the Great North Museum to give workshops and produce teaching and learning materials for the new National Curriculum that, thankfully, now requires children to learn about our earlier national history from the 'Stone Age to the Iron Age', an area that had previously been missing. This sweep of history maps perfectly over the range of periods that we unearthed at Low Hauxley and so we can use the site to provide a local example of this fascinating part of our past. Prehistory has always fascinated me and the site at Low Hauxley has undoubtedly

contained the longest archaeological sequence covering this period that I have ever excavated.

So what next? Well we know that there is still much that lies unexcavated at the site and that there will be many more remains as yet undiscovered that will eventually be eroded as the cliffs cut back. This erosion is a problem, and not just for Druridge Bay; it is a national problem affecting the entire British coastline.

As sea levels rise all the soft sediment cliffs will cut back and this means that archaeological sites in the intertidal and coastal zone will be destroyed. In recent years the timber circle known as 'Seahenge' was excavated at Holme-next-the-Sea off the Norfolk coast and at Ravenglass in Cumbria the western side of a Roman fort is eroding out of the cliff face. In the Severn Estuary Mesolithic footprints have been recorded in the intertidal muds whilst off the Isles of Scilly and the Orkneys underwater burial cairns and unattributable prehistoric structures respectively have been identified. These exciting discoveries are just a few out of many hundreds of sites

ure 77. The ertidal peat covered north Cresswell with mal footprints oss its surface.

that are at risk on an almost daily basis around Britain's shoreline. Because these remains are being eroded as a result of natural processes there is no statutory mechanism to fund recording work on them unless they are designated (that is, if they are Listed Buildings or Scheduled Monuments).

As the vast majority of the eroding sites are not designated this means that there is no mechanism in place for ensuring they get recorded or excavated prior to destruction. English Heritage has been pro-active in funding a strategic Rapid Coastal Zone Assessment to identify and prioritise all the known sites at risk around the English coastline and there are similar projects in Scotland and Wales. We now have the information of where the most threatened sites are and which are the most important, but there is still no mechanism for

systematically dealing with them. At a time when public expenditure is being reined in, our coastal heritage is competing with other very worthy demands on the public purse. This said, the erosion of the coastline and the loss of irreplaceable archaeological remains poses a serious problem and it is one that, perhaps, can be addressed through a combination of Heritage Lottery and Heritage Agency support combined with community volunteer action and long term monitoring, school participation and university support, together with involvement of the regional and national museums. The information gain and public good resulting from such a relatively modest financial outlay is potentially enormous and I hope that this project has sketched out a template that could be replicated elsewhere.

Figure 78. Erosion of the cliff face sediments continue on a daily basis with only a short window of opportunity to record them before they are lost.

RECOMMENDED READING

Beckensall, S. 2001. *Prehistoric Rock Art in Northumberland*. Stroud, Tempus.

Coles, B. 1998. Doggerland: A Speculative Survey. *Proceedings of the Prehistoric Society* 64: 45-8.

Frodsham, P. (ed.) 2004. *Archaeology in Northumberland National Park*. York, Council for British Archaeology Research Report 136.

Gaffney, V., Fitch, S. and Smith, D. 2009. *Europe's Lost World. The Rediscovery of Doggerland*. York, Council for British Archaeology Research Report 160.

Gamble, M. and Fowler, C. 2013. A re-assessment of Early Bronze Age human remains in Tyne and Wear Museums: results and implications for interpreting Early Bronze Age burials from North East England and beyond. *Archaeologia Aeliana* 5th ser. 42: 47–80.

Hodgson, N., McKelvey, J. and Muncaster, W. 2012. *The Iron Age on the Northumberland Coastal Plain. Excavations in Advance of Development 2002–2010*. Newcastle upon Tyne, Tyne & Wear Museums Archaeological Monograph No.3.

Passmore, D.G. and Waddington, C. 2012. *Archaeology and Environment in Northumberland. Till Tweed Studies Volume 2*. Oxford, Oxbow Books and English Heritage.

Sturt, F., Garrow, D. and Bradley, S. 2013. New Models of North West European Palaeogeography and Inundation. *Journal of Archaeological Science* 40 (11): 3963-3976.

Tolan-Smith, C. 2005. A cairn on Birkside Fell – excavations in 1996 and 1997. *Archaeologia Aeliana* 4th ser. 34: 55–65.

Tolan-Smith, C. 2008. Mesolithic Britain. In G.N. Bailey and P. Spikins (eds) *Mesolithic Europe*. Cambridge, Cambridge University Press: 132–57.

Waddington, C. 2007. Neolithic rock-art in the British Isles: retrospect and prospect. In A. Mazel, G. Nash and C. Waddington (eds) *Art as Metaphor: The Prehistoric Rock-Art of Britain*. Oxford, Archaeopress: 49–68.

Waddington, C. 2008. *Mesolithic Settlement in the North Sea Basin. A Case Study from Howick, North East England*. Oxford, Oxbow Books and English Heritage.

Waddington, C. and Passmore, D. 2004. Ancient Northumberland. Wooler, Country Store and English Heritage.

Waddington, C., Bailey, G., Boomer, I. and Milner, N. 2006. A Bronze Age cist cemetery at Howick, Northumberland. *Archaeological Journal* 162: 65–95.

About the Author

Clive Waddington has a 1st Class Honours Degree and MA from Newcastle University and a PhD from the University of Durham. He worked as a contract consultant for English Heritage and freelanced for various heritage institutions across the UK before taking up a lectureship at Newcastle University after which he established a commercial archaeological consultancy, Archaeological Research Services Ltd, which he continues to lead as Managing Director. He has published over 70 peer reviewed papers, books and book sections, appears frequently on television and radio and has given several hundred public and academic lectures throughout Britain and around the world.

Meet the Excavation Team

Clive	Chris	Dave	Jim
Joe	Kate	Kristian	Laura
Lucy	Philippa	Sophie	Steve